#CHILL

BRYAN E. ROBINSON, PH.D.

#CHILL

TURN OFF
YOUR JOB
AND TURN ON
YOUR LIFE

Thorsons

Thorsons
An imprint of HarperCollins*Publishers*
1 London Bridge Street
London SE1 9GF

www.harpercollins.co.uk

First published in the US by William Morrow, an imprint of
HarperCollins*Publishers* 2019
This UK edition published 2019

1 3 5 7 9 10 8 6 4 2

Printed and bound in Great Britain by
CPI Group (UK) Ltd, Croydon

MIX
Paper from
responsible sources
FSC™ C007454

This book is produced from independently certified FSC™ paper
to ensure responsible forest management.

For more information visit: www.harpercollins.co.uk/green

For my spouse, Jamey McCullers, the love
of my life and my favorite chill pill

CONTENTS

INTRODUCTION

In elementary school, the period I hated most was recess. When a teacher forgot to assign homework over Christmas vacation, I was the one who raised his hand to remind her. In high school, I wrote, directed, and produced the church Christmas play, designing and building the sets, and acting the lead role of Joseph. Doing *everything* gave me a sense of control missing within my chaotic family, where furniture-breaking fights between my mother and father were a regular occurrence.

In the throes of my adult work addiction, I needed my work—and hid it from others—the way my alcoholic father needed and hid his bourbon. And just as a child I tried to control my father's drinking by pouring out his booze and refilling the bottle with vinegar, the people who loved me pleaded and tore their hair out trying to keep me from working all the time.

Every summer just before we left on vacation, my spouse, Jamey, would search my bags and confiscate any work I planned to smuggle into our rented beach house on the South Carolina shore. But however thorough the search, Jamey always missed the tightly folded papers covered with work notes that I had stuffed into the pockets of my jeans.

When Jamey and our close friends invited me to stroll on the beach, I'd say I was tired and wanted to nap. While they were off swimming and playing in the surf, I secretly worked in the empty house, bent over a lap desk fashioned from a board. At the sound of returning footsteps, I stuffed my papers back into my jeans, hid the board, and stretched out on the bed, pretending to sleep.

It's only in hindsight that I can see I was a workaholic. Work was my sanctuary—my source of stability, self-worth, and protection against the uncertainties of life. I worked hard, yes, but I used work to defend myself against unwelcome emotional states—to modulate anxiety, sadness, and frustration. Jamey complained that I was never home—and that when I was, I didn't listen—but my university colleagues called me responsible and conscientious. I even toiled through most of the day of my father's funeral. While my mother and sisters broke bread with old neighbors, I was in my university office twenty-five miles away, working on a project so insignificant I no longer remember what it was. Jamey called me controlling, inflexible, and incapable of living in the moment—but the promotions, accolades, and fat paychecks built an ever-stronger case against his accusations. I used them to vilify him: *Why couldn't he pull his own weight? Why couldn't he be more supportive? Why was he constantly bothering me with problems that distracted me from building my career?*

My life was crumbling under my feet, and I couldn't do anything about it. Or so I thought. I didn't smile. I couldn't eat. I didn't care if I lived or died. Even with my first book published, with other great projects in the works—I was a chain-smoking, caffeine-drinking work junkie, dogged by self-doubt. I had no close friends. My memory got so bad, members of my family wondered if I was developing early-onset Alzheimer's. I snapped at colleagues, and they snapped back. I couldn't stop working.

When I entered counseling to "help Jamey with his problem," the therapist confronted me about my work addiction and work/life imbalance. I joined Workaholics Anonymous, entered therapy, and stumbled into yoga and meditation. But what ultimately brought me through the ordeal was the practice of *mindfulness meditation*—present-moment attention to my feelings and a compassionate, nonjudgmental connection with myself. The practice helped me begin my climb out of the work stupor into a saner life. And Jamey and I started to understand the crack in the foundation of our relationship.

I started to see my life through fresh eyes, watching Jamey care for his orchids and realizing the wisdom contained in the pleasure I got from simply working in the yard. As I started to chill, much to my surprise, I discovered how much I relished the smell of cut grass, the sight of a hummingbird pollinating a flower, the feel of warm earth between my fingers, and chats with neighbors.

Now instead of spending Saturdays in my basement office, I look forward to weekends of yard work, garage sales, and afternoon matinees with Jamey. When we go on vacation, I don't pretend to nap anymore. I fish by the dock, walk along the shore, and swim in the surf. Learning to be mindful of the present moment has enabled me to enjoy and savor my life as much as I had once savored my endless work.

#CHILL

JANUARY

I didn't need to use drugs because my bloodstream was manufacturing my own crystal meth.

—WORKAHOLICS ANONYMOUS MEMBER

FRESH STARTS

There are so many benefits to living a more chilled life. What better time to reevaluate and reset than January—the start of a new year with limitless possibilities? January is named for *Janus*, the Roman god of gates and doorways. There are many doorways and starting gates. And each of us begins from a different one, which raises the question: Is it possible for you to be nowhere else except *exactly* where you are? Or do you compare yourself to others and whisper inside that you should be further along in constructing a more chilled life? The important thing is for you to start the year from your own doorway. Nonstop working gets you lost in worry, stress, and anticipation, preventing you from seeing all of life's possibilities. Are you ready to admit that constant working has made your life a hot mess, that you are powerless over a whole host of factors and conditions? Are you ready to begin exploring from where you are to bring your life into greater balance with more time to chill? Are you willing to drop your judgments, expectations, and preconceived ideas and approach your life with fresh eyes?

In Buddhism, this is called Right Mindfulness, waking up from a life on automatic and becoming fully aware of the present moment. What better time

#CHILL

to start Right Mindfulness than with the "beginner's mind"—an expansive way of being in the world that opens you up to endless opportunities for your growth?

Two back-to-back heads symbolize the Roman god Janus, signifying that he is looking backward and forward at the same time. In this chapter, you have a chance to look back on your life and see that overworking has made it unmanageable. Looking forward, you contemplate ways to begin anew and build your life foundation around what matters most to you and make it more manageable. You become aware of what you have neglected and what needs attention for greater balance in the New Year: perhaps a faltering relationship, a healthier lifestyle, better work habits, a slower pace, or a generally more positive outlook.

CONSTRUCT YOUR SCAFFOLDING

Your workaholic habits are like an old building that needs renovating to withstand future wear and tear. As you conduct the repair work, you need temporary scaffolding—a wood plank to stand on and metal poles to lean on—until your foundation is steady.

Start by finding a quiet place to sit for five minutes. With eyes closed, silently ask yourself if you have sufficient structures in place to create fresh starts: A self-care plan? Workaholics Anonymous meetings? A counselor? Daily meditations?

If you haven't considered new scaffolding, contemplate what kind of support might bring you more balance in the New Year. The strategies you start with—much like physical scaffolding—are incrementally removed as you develop stamina to sustain healthy work/life balance on your own.

EMBRACE YOUR FLAWS

If someone were to ask you to make a list of your character defects, the list might reach the front door. It's so easy for you to see your shortcomings, and so difficult to see your worth. When you tend to see tiny individual flaws instead of an overall gleaming surface, it makes any success look and feel like failure.

Nothing truly beautiful is perfect. A flaw is the mark of being an imperfect human. Like all of us who are flawed, you're an imperfect human being doing the best you can—but understanding requires a shift in thinking.

Ask yourself what you need to do to embrace your flaws, to give yourself credit for your accomplishments. Then imagine putting your arms around your

JANUARY

flawed parts, accepting the things you cannot change, and changing those you can.

TURN OFF YOUR AUTOPILOT

Chances are you have lived your life on autopilot—not attuned to your surroundings or yourself. Perhaps you hit the ground running from the moment you wake up and then shake your fist at the clock because there aren't enough hours in the day.

When you frantically work on a project, worried the boss won't like the finished product or dreaming about the upcoming weekend, you're practicing *mindlessness*. The practice of *mindfulness*—the peaceful observing awareness of everything you do—takes you off autopilot. You can then tune in to your surroundings in a calm, compassionate way, and focus on what's happening right now. Whether it's weeding the garden or preparing dinner, cultivating mindful awareness of your daily activities, instead of placing an intense focus on the completion of the task, enriches your life.

SHUN WORK HIGHS

Work addiction has been called this century's cocaine. Workweeks of sixty, eighty, even a hundred hours are commonplace in major law firms and corporations. Workaholics take on more tasks than are possible to complete, toiling around the clock to juggle many balls in the air and rushing to meet tight deadlines. Many throw all-nighters, sleeping off work binges in their clothes.

Work highs run a cycle of adrenaline-charged binge working. Some say the surge of adrenaline pumping through your veins is a stronger stimulant than any other drug. Over time, if you're a workaholic, you require larger doses to maintain the original high. And then you put yourself—and those around you—under stress trying to reach that next high. Slowing down can be a buzzkill in the short term, but it pays off with a deeper, more satisfying type of high known as #chill.

Once your life becomes unmanageable, you need to take an honest inventory of work/life imbalance. Starting now, ask yourself, what healthy changes could you make to create more balance in your life?

WALK ONE STEP AT A TIME

No matter how challenging your workloads, you can find solace in the phrase "One step at a time." When life's burdens are too much to bear, when you struggle with indecision and too much responsibility, this powerful phrase helps you navigate the sea of work and family demands, self-imposed pressures, and emotional turmoil.

JANUARY

CHILL

Another important phrase is the Latin *festina lente*, translating to "make haste slowly"—move cautiously and step by step in work, love, and play. Most problems exist in yesterday or tomorrow. But yesterday is over, and tomorrow isn't here. All you have is this moment. You need to tackle only the things that demand resolution now. Tomorrow you can deal with tomorrow.

PRACTICE DEEP LISTENING

Maybe there are times when you're out of your body and don't listen because you're somewhere else. Do you do anything to keep from looking deeply within yourself? Do you finish other people's sentences to rush through a conversation? Are you so intent on getting your own point across that you don't hear the other person? Or are you back at work in your head finishing that report on your desk?

Deep listening happens when both parties are willing to communicate about problems and concerns. Both parties strive for a harmonious connection through empathy and respect for the other's point of view—without criticism, only love and compassion.

How do you measure up with deep listening? Are there specific tactics you can take to improve your listening abilities at work, home, and play? For example, instead of thinking of what you want to say next or hijacking the conversation to your point of view, try fully engaging in what another person says and feels. Use direct eye contact, don't give advice unless it's asked for, and reflect back what you hear with empathy by conveying what you imagine he or she must be feeling. And most important of all, stay mentally attuned with your body in the present moment instead of mentally going back to your workstation.

BEWARE FALSE THREATS

Mother Nature hardwired you to pay more attention to threats so you can survive. If you're a workaholic, you're doubly prone to work in a fight-or-flight mode. You predict negative outcomes about the future without proof—even when there's evidence to the contrary. In other words, you turn neutral or positive situations into negative ones.

This type of distorted thinking—called *fortune-telling*—is an unreliable source of information. To reduce this stressful outlook, start using your mind, instead of letting your mind abuse you.

The first step is to catch yourself making negative predictions, then ask if there's evidence. Finding evidence before jumping to conclusions saves you a lot of self-loathing, unnecessary worry, and valuable time. After dedicated practice, you begin to notice

JANUARY

#CHILL

a difference in your ability to think and feel more positively.

EMPOWER YOURSELF

Who have you empowered to take charge of your work life? Who do you allow to judge you on the adequacy of your toil? When you tell yourself that you need more hours in the day, that you should or you have to or you can't, you become a victim of the situation.

But you're not at the mercy of the work world. You just think you are. It's essential to reach a place within you where frantic rushing, adrenaline surges, and fatigue no longer feel normal. No matter how stressed and overwhelming work becomes, you always have the freedom to choose how you respond to difficult situations. And work demands can't take away that liberty unless you allow them to.

Here are a few ideas for daily empowerment:

- Instead of reacting immediately to that nonurgent but really difficult email, take a deep breath, step away from your workstation, and treat yourself to a brief walk or your favorite beverage.

- When bad news hits, focus on the upside of the downside situation. "I have to pay a fortune in taxes" becomes "I made more money this year than ever before."

- When under pressure, bring to mind in vivid detail a time you handled a challenge with confidence and courage and notice your muscles relax, heart rate drop, and breathing slow.

PINPOINT OPPORTUNITIES

When you're stressed, your mind targets the negative threat instead of looking for a positive opportunity within the problem. If you're searching for a solution to a crisis, your negative emotions keep you focused on the problem. Without realizing it, you block out the opportunity.

Positivity leads you toward more possibilities, automatically lifting your work stress. A positive scope widens your worldview, changes your outlook, and allows you to take in more information that can lead to better solutions.

In order to pinpoint opportunities contained in negative situations, try asking, "How can I make this situation work to my advantage?" or "What can I manage, learn, or overcome in this instance?"

STOP THE BLAME GAME

How often do you blame others for your shortcomings or foul moods? When things don't go as planned, try looking deeply inside yourself and look for the real reasons.

JANUARY

CHILL

No matter how often you blame others, it will not change whatever it is about you that makes you unhappy. The main thing blame does is distract you from taking an honest look at yourself as you search for external reasons to explain your discontent.

Every time you blame coworkers or family members for your work frustrations or failures, you prevent yourself from healing your work addiction. Looking deeper within yourself with compassion and committing to owning your actions, lifts you from workplace adolescence to workplace maturity.

OVERRIDE NEGATIVITY BIAS

Scientists say that everyone is susceptible to a negativity bias that causes you to overestimate life's obstacles and underestimate your ability to conquer them. When you're constantly in survival mode, no wonder it's a challenge for you to achieve work/life balance!

But there's good news, too. The secret is to underestimate challenges and overestimate your ability to handle them. Scientists say it takes three positive thoughts to offset one negative thought. With a little practice, you can override your mind's knee-jerk negativity and activate your rest-and-digest response. It's time to look at work demands as an adventure to experience and consider setbacks as lessons to learn from instead of failures to endure.

EMBRACE MAYBE

Things don't always go as planned. Life will go awry and unexpected events will blindside you. Maybe it rains on the picnic you're having. The car stalls in traffic. A cold puts you out of commission. You won't always get the promotion. Life is not on your time schedule, and you don't get to tailor it to your needs. It tailors you to its needs.

Work addiction counts on certainty and predictability. It wants you to know what, who, when, where, and how things will happen. Otherwise, you freak out.

Being okay with not having a definite outcome offers you comfort from your rigid expectations. It loosens you up to the fact that for every possibility, there are numerous ways a situation can resolve.

LEARN TO ENJOY WAITING

My guess, because you're reading this book, is that you might have difficulty waiting for solutions to problems. Perhaps you look for quick answers to rush to closure and often make impulsive decisions so you can get to the next item on the agenda.

If the right decision were nestled inside an egg, you couldn't force the egg to hatch. Important work decisions are like that, too. They don't come when you force them. Outside-the-box solutions tend to appear while you are doing other things—vacuuming or rearranging your desk—because they need the opportunity to hatch on their own.

Chilled workers hold two opposing opinions or decisions simultaneously without making impulsive choices. You gather all the facts before starting projects and avoid mistakes by conducting research and weighing decisions with reflection until the best solution emerges. Once you learn to enjoy waiting, you don't mind waiting to enjoy.

ALLOW WIGGLE ROOM

Chances are you don't leave wiggle room between work tasks, scheduling back-to-back appointments so tightly that you don't have cushions for life's surprises—or even bathroom breaks. You use extra time between tasks to cross one more item off the list instead of taking a deep breath, relaxing, and showing up a few minutes early.

Lack of wiggle room has you constantly under the gun, dashing from one commitment to the next. When life throws a curveball—traffic congestion, family crisis, or health problem—you get overwhelmed and stressed out.

You can drastically reduce this stress by creating comfortable margins. When you focus on chilling, you can use windshield time to decompress from daily pressures, play enjoyable music, and focus on relaxing instead of chewing over the events of the day.

PRACTICE SELF-ACCEPTANCE

Chances are you're such a stickler that few people—not even you—can meet your standards. While chilled workers set goals of 95 to 100 percent, overachievers set unrealistic goals of 150 percent. When you fall short, your ego berates you mercilessly to make sure you get it "right" next time. Problem is, even the next time isn't good enough for perfectionists like you.

This type of inner abuse fuels work addiction. Unable to accept that you cannot measure up to your own impossible standards, you push to work harder and longer, neglecting everything and everyone, to go deeper into performing and achieving.

Once you learn to accept yourself—with your flaws and fallibility—you're able to make mistakes without self-condemnation but with self-acceptance. This practice opens you to creative ideas that make you a better worker, colleague, and family member. Con-

JANUARY

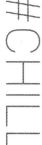

template giving up being perfect, working on becoming yourself, and expressing yourself in ways that are natural to you.

AVOID MULTITASKING

If you're like many overscheduled people, you consider multitasking to be an essential survival tool in a 24/7-work culture that expects immediate results. Performing one activity at a time just feels underproductive.

Studies show that multitasking isn't what it's cracked up to be. Juggling emails and text messages undermines your ability to focus and produce, fatiguing your brain in the process. Multitasking also undermines efficiency and quality of life. It often results in half-baked projects that leave you overwhelmed and stressed out.

Once in a while you must perform more than one activity at a time. But you can put the brakes on multitasking so it doesn't become your normal course of action. You can prioritize and engage in fewer tasks at one time. You can slow down your pace and finish one project before starting another.

INVEST IN LOVED ONES

When work becomes more important than anything else, you develop a pattern of forgetting, ignoring, or

minimizing the importance of family rituals and celebrations. You miss your child's final bow. You forget
the birthday party. And even if you do make it to an
event, you might have trouble concentrating because
your mind is back at the office.

What did you miss because you were working?
Was it that school play or your daughter's winning
shot? It's important to contemplate what is conveyed
to your family when work always comes first. Consider your work and change the patterns that don't
support your family priorities.

RECOGNIZE DENIAL

Chances are people tell you that you work too much.
Perhaps loved ones say you never have time for them,
a colleague says you're the first to arrive and last to
leave work, or friends say they don't see you anymore.

If you died tomorrow, would you be content with
the way you're living? Maybe if you look and listen to
the cues from others, you could learn that nonstop
working has fooled you all along, that you've taken
its lies for truth. Denial is part of the disease of work
addiction that says if you relax you'll fall behind or
something bad will happen. Or you trick yourself into
believing you're just trying to make an honest living
for your family. Truth be told, you're doing it for your-

self to medicate an inner condition. I suggest that you inventory the amount of time and energy you put into interests outside work. Then without self-judgment, identify what you've neglected and give it more attention.

SIT WITH IT

You probably are in the habit of ignoring unpleasant situations or problems that stew inside. Staying busy takes your mind off worry. While escapes dampen the flames of unrest and bring temporary relief, they don't fix the mental burdens over the long haul.

In taking you away from the present moment, distractions eclipse your clarity and self-understanding. Quieting your mind through meditation, paying attention to your mental worries and burdens that you carry inside, and sitting with them in full nonjudgmental awareness calms down the beginner's mind.

As an experiment, the next time an unsettling feeling or sense of unrest pops up, go inward, welcome the feeling, and sit with it. As you connect in the present moment, get to know this part of you with as much compassion as possible. Don't try to change the feelings but simply sit with them as you might provide bedside company for a sick friend. That's it. Be present with the unpleasantness, bringing as much awareness as possible. Each time a thought or body sensation pulls you away, try gently bringing your attention back again. After a while, life seems to run more smoothly.

LET IT GO

Like many of us, the adults in your life might have taught you that holding on and fighting against opposition are signs of great strength. The paradox is that holding on and resisting can be signs of great ignorance. Would you fight against a dangerous riptide pulling you out to sea if you knew fighting it would drown you? In this and many of life's instances, it takes more strength and courage to let go and relax.

Letting go doesn't mean giving up. You let go of controlling the things you can't control or don't need to control. When you let go, you win the world. You stop sweating the small stuff, making mountains out of molehills, and start rolling with life's punches. You focus on the big battles instead of the little ones and let life happen on its own terms instead of trying to make it fit into yours.

DON'T BE A MARTYR

Are you a workaholic martyr who refuses to delegate and assumes more than your share of the workload—even refusing to take earned vacation time? Do you

JANUARY

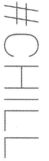

blame the workplace, whine about administrative honchos, or complain that colleagues don't work as hard as you? If so, by doing this, you victimize yourself and lose your empowerment, walking around with the world on your shoulders—a burden that you put there.

Perhaps it's time to question whether your bad habits or negative attitudes contribute to job problems, and consider how to take responsibility for your part. What actions can you take? Say no more often? Delegate? Prioritize? Work more efficiently? Speak to someone in authority who can help? Resign?

BE MINDFUL OF YOUR ZINGERS

Suppose you hit your head on a kitchen cabinet. After the first zinger of pain comes the second zinger of judgment: "Ouch! I'm such a klutz!" When you fail at something, make a mistake, or have a setback, the second zinger of self-judgment creates another layer of stress, making you feel bad. It's the second zinger, the stress you put on yourself, that causes suffering. If you can remove the second layer of judgment, you feel at ease to deal with the real stressor.

Next time you get zinged, pay attention to your second zinger and observe yourself without judgment. This is called *equanimity*—the ability to stay calm amid a distressful situation. Attaining equanimity isn't as easy as it sounds, but it's a challenge worth the effort. You realize you don't have to react with second zingers every time you get zinged and that it's possible to chill under almost any circumstances.

FILL YOUR EMOTIONAL BANK

Truth be told, saying yes to all requests sends a constant no to yourself and prevents you from meaningful work. The ability to say no isn't a weakness or failure. It's a character strength.

Think of yourself as a bank account. When overworking or caretaking withdrawals outweigh self-care, it's time to invest in your well-being. The key to avoid burnout is to make daily deposits by saying no when you're already overloaded, making sure to get ample rest, exercise, and nutrition, and prioritizing what interests and replenishes you. When you take care of yourself first, you have more energy to invest in business and personal pursuits later on. What can you say no to in order to concentrate on creating more work/life balance? Contemplate what daily deposits you could make to equal the withdrawals that yes takes from your personal account. Then ask, "How do I start?"

JANUARY

#CHILL

USE ANTIFREEZE

The compulsion to do overpowers your desire to be. You keep your feelings on ice to defend yourself from unwelcome emotional states—like anxiety, sadness, and frustration. Immersion in work gives you safety and security regardless of whether the work itself is satisfying.

As you start to commit to a more balanced life, you move from human doing to human being. You notice your feelings of anxiety start to thaw, and you feel more tenderness toward yourself and others. You lose some of your control and perfectionism, finding other avenues through which to value yourself.

Seeking solace in work allows you to avoid relationship conflicts and to engage in an activity you can control and feel safe. Constant work keeps you numb, your feelings buried in the deep freeze and emotionally disconnected from others. In this New Year, it's time for you to get curious about what inside needs thawing.

LOOK IN THE MIRROR

Once a stranger approached a farmer working in the field and said, "I've been thinking of moving and wondered what kind of people live around here." The farmer asked, "What kind of people live where you come from?" The stranger said, "They're selfish and mean and not friendly at all. I'll be glad to leave them behind." The farmer replied, "I expect you'll find the same sort of people around here, too. You won't like it here." The stranger went on.

Later in the day another stranger came along and said to the farmer, "I've been thinking of moving and wondered what kind of people live in this area." The farmer asked, "What kind of people live where you come from?" The stranger answered, "Wonderful people. They're generous and kind and very friendly. I'll be sorry to leave them." The farmer replied, "Well, I expect you'll find the same sort of people around here, too: generous and kind and very friendly. I believe you'll like it here."

The faults of others are like automobile headlights that seem more glaring than your own. When you react negatively to someone, you often are reacting to something within yourself that you don't like. Focusing on the faults of others is a way to distract you from acknowledging what you need to work on in yourself.

CARPE DIEM

As you ponder your own mortality, you realize how fleeting life is. Instead of focusing on what went wrong today or worrying what might happen tomorrow, re-

JANUARY

flect on how you're living: back-to-back meetings, cell phones ringing after hours, mounds of work on weekends. Think about the ones you love and ask, "Am I living my daily life in concert with what's most important to me?"

Carpe Diem—Latin for seize the day—reminds you to live your life fully and get important business done. Perhaps today is the time to tell someone "I love you," make a confession, or mend a relationship. Maybe it's time to seize the day to do what you have left undone or haven't yet started.

ADMIT POWERLESSNESS

In Step 1 of Workaholics Anonymous, you admit you're powerless over work addiction and that your life has become unmanageable. Admitting powerlessness removes the roadblock of know-it-all superiority. Through this admission, you acknowledge your human fallibility and humility. This is the basis for admitting you're human, allowed to make mistakes, and cannot do everything yourself. No matter how hard you try you cannot control the world and the people in it. You leave the actual workings of your life to a universe that is more powerful than you are. It's counterintuitive, but when you can admit that you're powerless over the ability to

manage your compulsive work habits, you feel empowered to surmount the problem.

You are only one person and cannot do everything,
but still you can do something. Although you're limited
in the things you can control, you don't refuse to do
what will lead to a healthy, productive life.

JANUARY TAKEAWAYS

- Put temporary scaffolding in place until you have
  confidence and the emotional stamina to move
  forward on your own with greater work/life
  balance.
- Monitor the overpowering urge to overload
  yourself.
- Acknowledge that overworking has made your
  life unmanageable.
- Practice moment-to-moment reflection of your
  inner life and deep listening while being fully
  present with what's happening around you.
- Learn to admit your flaws and to embrace each
  one without judgment.
- Accept the things you cannot change and change
  the things you can.
- Seize the day to live mindfully and fully in the
  present so that tomorrow brings no regrets.

JANUARY

FEBRUARY

A chilled worker sits in the office dreaming of being on the ski slopes. A workaholic stands on the ski slopes dreaming about being back in the office.

HEARTSPEAK AND COMPASSION

Traditionally the month of February, derived from the Latin term *februum* for the purification ritual *Februa,* was a time of cleansing. Many people say that mid-February is hands-down the most depressing time of the year. The days are short, it's cold and gloomy, and people tend to isolate from the inclement weather. But February is also known as the month of love—a time to remember the importance of compassion—toward others as well as yourself.

How often do regrets of the past or worries of the future cause you to hide in your work? If you're blue during the winter months, one of the best ways to chill your mind is to find a source of strength greater than yourself, to purify your mood and to help you remember you're not alone. A spiritual figure, a close confident, a counselor, an online Workaholics Anonymous meeting, or a sponsor can restore purpose and meaning beyond hyperbusyness and working too much.

The practice of self-compassion and lovingkindness toward others actually boosts a low mood. Performing kind acts gives you a break to chill from your own burdens and connects you to other people, while giving you a sense of purpose, self-worth, and euphoria, commonly known as the "helper's high."

In this chapter, you come to understand the power of lovingkindness and how it leads to a healthier, more balanced life. You discover that you're more in charge of your mind and that it's less in charge of you. Your heartspeak cleanses you of angry and resentful thoughts. It helps you realize that most people who make you miserable—a neighbor's barking dog, the shopper who unknowingly steps in front of you in line, or the swimmer who splashes you with a belly dive—are like you: human beings, likely doing the best they can, and that a piece of you resides in every person you encounter.

BECOME MORE MINDFUL

How many people do you notice driving while texting or eating lunch while pounding away at a keyboard? Perhaps you're one of them. On autopilot, regretful of past actions or worried about future outcomes, stampeding over the present moment as if it were an obstacle in the way of your deadline or the next item on the agenda? If so, your mind is using you instead of you using it.

Mindfulness practices show you how to take charge of your mind. Through this practice, you bring present-moment attention to what's happening inside you and learn to focus on treating others and yourself with lovingkindness.

In a comfortable place with eyes open or closed, bring your full attention to the thoughts streaming through your mind without attempting to change them. Simply observe the thoughts for five minutes much as you might watch a leaf floating along a brook. Then notice what you're aware of in your mind and body and how the exercise makes you feel.

LISTEN TO YOUR HEART

When you come into the world, love is who you are at your core. Pure love. Over time you get hurt and put up walls and defenses to help you survive this thing called life. You find ways to avoid or escape from further heartbreak by working yourself to death. You think you have everything under control, but your heart remains closed to tenderness.

Love is still who you are. You can tell it's there by the swelling of your heart when your oldest graduates or your youngest makes the winning shot. The flood of tears when you lose someone you hold dear. To open yourself to vulnerability, look deeper and find

FEBRUARY

\#CHILL

your heartspeak. Find the things and experiences that move you beyond words, and you'll see yourself approaching life with more sensitivity and loving-kindness.

GIMME FIVE

When work or daily tasks are the most important priorities, you miss out on the amazing moments of life. Is this really the way you want to continue to live? Whooshing through life wearing blinders, tied to outcomes?

What would it be like if you nudged a few agenda items out of the way temporarily and savored a few present moments? I'm not talking about long periods of time, just five minutes out of the 1,440 minutes in a day to get a taste of what's around you. You can't use the excuse that somewhere between sunrise and sunset you don't have five precious minutes to chill. That still leaves 1,435 minutes a day to get business done. Isn't it worth five present minutes to connect with the way the morning dew glimmers on a spider web, the smell of chimney smoke swirling across a winter moon, or sounds of chirping birds on your windowsill and let life replenish you?

HALT

The acronym HALT stands for "hungry, angry, lonely, or tired." When work addiction overtakes you and pulls you out of your life, this alert signal can bring you back into balance. If one or a combination of the four states is present, HALT is a gentle reminder for you to stop or slow down.

It's a memory device for when you're drowning in work woes, and reminds you to take a few breaths and chill. First, take a deep abdominal breath through your nose. Hold it while you count to six. Then purse your lips and exhale slowly through them.

Act intentionally to take care of yourself: eat when hungry, let out your anger in a constructive way, call someone if you're lonely, and rest when you're tired.

AVOID MAKING ASSUMPTIONS

Suppose your boss walks by your desk. You smile and nod. She doesn't acknowledge you, so you wonder what you've done wrong to get on her bad side. Later you discover she had a lot on her mind and wasn't even aware of your presence.

Automatically accepting negative thoughts and fears as fact creates unnecessary problems. You can save yourself a lot of needless suffering by questioning

FEBRUARY

automatic thoughts and waiting to see if the evidence supports them. As you practice this approach, you learn not to trust your assumptions. It's better to suspend your conclusions and wait to connect the dots once you have asked questions or confirmed the facts.

DON'T BE SCARED OF BEING VULNERABLE

Excessive working seems to cocoon you and keep you safe, but it also disconnects you from people. Making yourself vulnerable requires sticking your neck out and taking emotional risks: sharing your honest feelings, speaking your truth, and apologizing when you've done wrong.

The longest journey you will make is the eighteen inches between your head and heart. It's risky opening up on the inside—pulling back the curtain and allowing a friend, family member, or coworker to see your heart. But the healing that heartspeak gives you can be worth the risk.

FOREGO GOBBLE, GULP, AND GO

Did you know that the average American spends only eleven minutes eating a lunch at a fast-food restaurant? What about you? Are you a mindless eater, someone who grabs a pastry and gobbles it down with gulps of coffee as you rush out the door?

A well-nourished body has a stronger stress-resistance shield and fosters sustainability in the workplace. Whatever you put into your mouth and your frame of mind when you eat influence the quality of what comes out of your brain. It's time to balance your busy schedule and treat eating as a singular activity to enjoy for its own sake, just as you would an important work project.

EXPRESS GRATITUDE

The problem with constant wanting is that desire expands, and wanting increases discontentment. It fuels your work addiction so you can obtain things that help you feel better inside. Perhaps you overspend, overindulge, and overdo, but sooner or later there will be something you want but can't have, no matter how hard you work.

You can change this pattern with a more reliable approach to contentment: to feel grateful for what you already possess. Start by making a list of the many things that make life worth living, and visualize things you have taken for granted that, if you didn't have them, would leave your life empty and unfulfilling.

FEBRUARY

CHILL

STOP DUMPSTER-DIVING

Chances are you're so comfortable with castigating yourself for your shortcomings that it wouldn't even occur to you that a more positive, self-compassionate approach might make you a more effective worker. So you clobber yourself with criticism out of fear of becoming a slacker.

Dumpster-diving for faults only sabotages your success. While it's important to recognize your limitations and failures, it's also essential to appreciate your successes, be proud of your strengths, and treat yourself with courtesy and consideration.

LET THE GHOST GO

Self-doubt is a cruel ghost that can haunt you day and night. It stalks you when you have a big day on the job and lurks over your shoulder when you're presenting a huge project or trying to mend an important relationship.

A measure of doubt is a good thing to have. It's a form of checks and balances helping you get to the truth. It pushes you to question your goals rather than naïvely move forward with blinders on. In the extreme, however, self-doubt can be debilitating, especially if you believe that criticism helps you achieve goals.

The best approach is to treat yourself as you would a

loved one. During high-pressure workdays, mentoring yourself with pep talks and kind words spares you a lot of stress, calms you down, and carries you through the ups and downs. You can acknowledge uncertain thoughts—not to second-guess but to mindfully use them to benefit your daily balance.

LEARN YOUR LOVE LANGUAGE

February is a perfect time for love. A perfect time for you to ask yourself, "Am I truly loving the person I care about?" If you're in an intimate relationship, chances are you and your partner speak different love languages.

Some people feel loved when a partner spends quality time with them or affirms them with compliments. Others feel loved when that partner gives a gift or performs an act of service such as cooking a good meal. Still others feel loved by physical touch, such as hugs and holding hands.

What tells you that others love you? What are some things you do naturally to show your love for others? Answers to these questions can give you a picture of your love language and that of your partner. The next step is to share your discovery and practice speaking each other's love language on a regular basis. What a great Valentine's present to give each other.

FEBRUARY

AVOID BEING A SHOOTING STAR

While corporate America extols the virtues of work-aholism, studies show that it leads to inefficiency and erodes trust throughout the organization. It's not unusual for workaholics to generate a crisis and then to get attention and praise for resolving it.

If you're a workaholic, you become addicted to the process of working instead of getting the job done. Sometimes the amount of effort you put into projects exceeds the level of productivity. Optimal performers are more efficient and put in fewer work hours. They have warm, collegial interactions, have a good collaborative sense, and have mastered the art of delegating. They're motivated by a desire to make creative contributions and take more necessary risks to achieve positive, creative outcomes.

The career trajectories of workaholics are like shooting stars, rising quickly on the basis of a big splash then leveling off. If you're consumed with managing the details of your career, it's never too late to make a U-turn and change your approach. You can delegate, prioritize, and learn not to overload yourself. Instead of getting bogged down with details, you look at the big picture. And instead of covering up your mistakes, you become a master of self-correction and learn from them.

LET'S GET PHYSICAL

If you're like most people, you pay more attention to your automobile than to your body. You wash and wax your car, get it tuned up, make sure it has plenty of gas.

On the job, you have plenty of fuel, enough to push subordinates and yourself to finish designated assignments within unrealistic deadlines, spreading fear and havoc throughout the workplace. Your body is jet propelled, but what kind of attention and care do you give it when you're changing tires and going eighty miles per hour?

Chances are you're so accustomed to living in your body that you don't know it as well as you do your vehicle. If there's a rattle under the hood of a car, you check it out, but you don't pay much attention to physical signs of burnout. And you probably steamroll over aches and pains or ignore a reduced ability to function that warns of serious health problems.

The difference between your car and your body? Unless you're homeless, you live inside your body. It's important to know what it's up to and listen to what it's trying to tell you. So get physical and start appreciating the vehicle that houses and transports you wherever you want to go.

FEBRUARY

LIGHTEN YOUR DARK SPOTS

A colleague once told me that a client handed her a crisp hundred-dollar bill to pay for his therapy session. After he left, she realized he had mistakenly given her two hundred-dollar bills stuck together. Her first thought was, "I can keep this extra money, and nobody will ever know." But she chased him down and returned the extra bill.

It's important to take a look at the flipside of who you think you are. Ask yourself if you're afraid to examine the shadows in your personality. Or would you rather spend a lot of time denying the dark spots? Part of recovering from work addiction is being willing to acknowledge the loved ones, friends, and coworkers whom you've harmed. You can do it, not with self-condemnation but with self-compassion, so that you can see the broad scope of who you are.

RIDE THE CURRENT

Kayakers say the best way to escape when trapped in a hydraulic—a turbulent, funnel-shaped current—is to relax, and it will spit you out. But your natural tendency in the heat of the moment is to fight against the current, and that keeps you stuck, even drowns you.

In the same vein, the way to get unstuck from a torrent of negative thoughts streaming through your mind is to welcome and watch each thought with curiosity. This is counterintuitive, but when you let thoughts come and go without personalizing them, resisting them, or identifying with them, they eventually float away.

Think of a negative thought you've carried. Then hold the thought away from you and observe it for a few moments through a dispassionate eye. As you watch the thought, you start to realize it doesn't have to define you. It is not you, and it is not even necessarily true. And the bad feelings recede.

GET COMFORTABLE WITH REJECTION

People-pleasing is a direct result of insecurities and a tragic forfeiting of your own voice. The result? Everyone likes you but yourself.

When you try to appease everyone, it's only a matter of time before you lose yourself in those expectations. It's a fact of life that someone—or many people—will become angry or displeased with you. The key is to get comfortable with rejection, stop selling out for the approval of others, and be forthright in your opinions. It's important to take a stand and learn to disagree. This takes loads of courage but lands you in a happier state of mind and a more stable work/life balance.

FEBRUARY

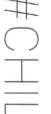

QUIT BEING A BYSTANDER

Raise your hand if you ever get the feeling that your life is passing you by from one workday to the next. Most of you? I thought so. Now, raise your hand if you think that, on your deathbed, you'll remember the time you spent working in the office. Few of you? I thought so.

Suppose you were asked, If you had your life to live over, what would you do differently? What would you say? Talk less, listen more? Would you invite friends over even though the carpet was stained and the sofa faded? Would you go to bed when you're sick instead of worry that the earth would go into a holding pattern if you miss work? Would there be more "I love you," more "I'm sorry"? Contemplate what comes up inside you as you ponder these questions.

AFFIRM YOURSELF

It's important to learn to work without external affirmations and to evaluate yourself with a dispassionate eye. Once you can do that, you're no longer dependent on external circumstances to build you up, and you can have a healthier relationship to your work. By recognizing your worth, you become a buttress of your self-esteem, built from the inside, a chilled worker, and master of your own fate.

Starting now, affirm yourself for a job well done. Replace fault-finding with favor-finding so your short-comings don't overshadow your accomplishments. Remember to affirm your strong points on a regular basis.

STOP CHEATING ON YOUR LIFE

In the progressive throes of work addiction, it wouldn't be unusual for you to hide work everywhere, despite complaints by family and friends: in briefcases or luggage, backpacks, under car seats, in dirty laundry bags, or stuffed inside pants. If you're like many work-aholics, you hide your work and sneak around or blow up at people who get in your way—in either situation, you're engaging in work infidelity.

Bootlegging work—similar to alcoholics hiding bottles of gin—is a sign of desperation. You must get your fix at all costs even if it means being dishonest or hurting the people you love most. From a workaholic's vantage point, concealment lowers tensions in the family, but loved ones feel betrayed and mistrustful once the truth is revealed. And relationships suffer severe, sometimes irreparable damage.

When your addiction to work is so strong that you're powerless over its pull, it's time to ask: "Why does

deception have such power and control over me?"
Honesty frees you from self-deception and teaches
you to admit your wrongs and to forgive yourself.

FIND YOUR PASSION

Passionate workers are motivated by intrinsic needs
and the desire to make creative contributions. They
are creative risk takers, stretching beyond customary
bounds to build ideas.

Workaholics, on the other hand, envision work
as a haven in a dangerous, emotionally unpredictable world. On a cellular level, passionate workers
operate from their rest-and-digest response while
workaholics operate on the fight-or-flight response,
which leads to a drench of cortisol and adrenaline that
compromises the immune system and leads to heart
disease, diabetes, and gastrointestinal problems.
Passionate workers are masters of self-correction
and learn from their mistakes. Workaholics try to
avoid or cover up mistakes.

You can ask yourself if you work from passion or
stress. When your mental and physical health is at
stake, your rest-and-digest response can create
a soothing, calmer approach to work tasks and a
greater satisfaction on the job.

DON'T LET THE LETDOWN GET YOU DOWN

A Chinese farmer had an old horse for tilling his fields. One day the horse escaped into the hills. When all the farmer's neighbors sympathized with the old man over his bad luck, he replied, "Bad luck? Good luck? Who knows?" A week later the horse returned with a herd of wild horses from the hills. This time the neighbors congratulated the farmer on his good luck. His reply, again, was, "Good luck? Bad luck? Who knows?" When the farmer's son was attempting to tame one of the wild horses, he fell off its back and the boy broke his leg. Everyone thought this was very bad luck. Not the farmer, whose only reply was, "Bad luck? Good luck? Who knows?" Weeks later, the army marched into the village and conscripted every able-bodied man they could find to go to war. When they saw the farmer's son with his broken leg, they let him off. Now, was that good luck? Bad luck? Who knows?

Things are rarely as bad as they seem. Our blessings often appear to us in the shape of pain, loss, or disappointment. If you remind yourself of this, you can always find a granule of good in the bad, gains in your losses. The next time you're in the middle of a letdown, you can uplift yourself by remembering that good or bad luck isn't in the situation; it resides in your

#CHILL

interpretation and is rarely as bad or as good as you imagine.

MODERATE EXPECTATIONS

There's an old saying batted around in recovery circles that expectations are premeditated resentments. Perhaps you have expectations of how situations will play out. When things don't go your way because of unexpected events, it naturally hurts and disappoints. But expecting a situation to be a certain way causes you to have a closed mind about the outcome. And if it doesn't conform to your mindset, you might throw a fit. This is self-will in disguise at its worse.

Once you start seeing that stance as immature, you realize the world operates on its own terms and that many things cannot be changed no matter what. Regardless of how hard you try, you cannot make the world and the people in it serve your will.

If you're overly controlling, you can learn that it's not your mission to bring order to the world. Your mission is to align yourself in unison with that world. You cannot eliminate life's disappointments, but you can choose how you respond to them by maturely accepting and making the best of the situation.

REMOVE THOSE WIRELESS LEASHES

There was a time when "Blackberries" were something *you* consumed, not something that consumed *you*. And when you had a "Bluetooth," you went to the dentist. The phrase "24/7," household slang of the twenty-first century, has replaced the "nine-to-five" adage of yore. These trends indicate how work has slithered its way into every hour of the day and your wireless leashes have become choker collars. They do permit you to bend over a laptop on an island in paradise or call the office via cell phone from the ski lift. But allowing wireless intrusions to call the shots can put you in a footrace that leaves you harried.

As the workday continues to invade your private space, you face the challenge of keeping a close watch on your personal life, moving at a reasonable pace, and staying connected to others in a compassionate, human way. It's up to you to draw the line. You don't leave a hammer or saw out after you've worked on a cabinet; you put the tools away. The same can be true for your wireless devices. How well do you walk the line between work intrusion and personal time? Ask yourself whether you're a line breaker or a line backer. Then consider what you could do to create more time to chill.

FEBRUARY

LET YOURSELF BE HIGHER POWERED

You fly solo when you power up with self-will, forcing your life to go the way you want it to go. Step 2 of Workaholics Anonymous teaches you that belief in a Power greater than yourself can restore you to a more balanced life.

On your own you can never know all that is needed to keep you aloft. But your belief in a Power greater than yourself helps you soar. When you allow the greater power of the universe to navigate, you face each day with renewed faith and courage. You're filled with inner strength to overcome obstacles and serenity is yours.

This power can be a God of your understanding, the Higher Power of a sunset or some other aspect of nature, the universe, an on-line Workaholics Anonymous meeting, or a power you find in a support group. The point is to believe that there is a greater power beyond your ego, and that can be whatever you rely on for your source of strength.

FEBRUARY TAKEAWAYS

- Remember to HALT when you are feeling overwhelmed.

- Unplug from your electronic devices once in a while to enjoy life's other pleasures.

- Identify your love language and those of the important people in your life to improve your intimate connections.

- Make it a habit to name your "tallcomings" when you list your shortcomings so you have a more balanced picture of who you really are.

- Look for the upside of every bad situation so the letdown doesn't hold you down.

- Connect with a Power greater than you so your ego doesn't call the shots.

MARCH

Happiness cannot be found through great effort and willpower, but is already here, right now, in relaxation and letting go.

—LAMA GENDUN RINPOCHE

LETTING GO AND SURRENDERING

In the North Carolina mountains, we have a saying: "When treed by a bear, enjoy the view." This advises that the best way to chill is to let go of your attachment to an outcome and make the best of an uncontrollable situation. If you're like most high performers, the negative thoughts running through your mind trap you into believing they are true, simply because they're in your head, even though they snare you into unhealthy feelings and bad decisions. You create suffering and exhaustion when your thoughts demand that a situation be different than it is, and you spend a lot of time upset over things you cannot control—forcing, resisting, and clinging to your self-will.

The month of March, named after Mars, the ultimate Roman warrior of heroic actions, comes in like a roaring lion with biting cold and often unpleasant, windy weather. March inspires you to muster the strength and courage of a roaring lion or hero warrior like Mars so you can let go of excessive work habits and surrender to situations beyond your control.

Surrendering and letting go are actions of personal strength and power—not defeat. When you're able to step back and chill, you realize that negative thoughts are prison bars that eclipse your ability to see all of life's possibilities. It takes the strength and courage of a roaring lion or Roman warrior to surrender your control to unknown situations and allow life to happen on its terms.

In this chapter, you develop a lion's courage to let go of the narrow blinders you were taught to wear that reduce your visibility of the big picture and blur your clarity. You start to go wide and replace your zoom lens with a wide-angle one, freeing yourself from tightly held beliefs, feelings, or actions. Then you envision a broader range of positive options in your life. The end result? You come into March like a lion and go out like a lamb—still courageous and powerful but now warm, springlike, and docile—balanced with peace and serenity.

STRESS LESS

If your life is fast-paced and hard-driven, you're probably out of touch with your body. You're unaware of the stress that builds and ignore soreness, aches, and pains, overly focusing on the business of the day. As a result, you tend to abuse your body instead of taking care of it. *Pendulation* is an exercise that teaches you to focus on your physical body.

With your eyes closed, notice a place in your body where you feel stress. It can show up as pain, tension, an ache, or constriction. Then swing your attention to a place inside where you feel less stress or no stress. Focus on the absence of stress, noticing your bodily sensations: steady heartbeat, slowed breathing, warm skin, softened jaw, relaxed muscles. Then imagine the sensation of the absence of stress spreading to other parts of your body.

Now shift back to the place where you originally felt stress. If the sensation has decreased, focus on the reduction of tension for a few minutes. Continue moving your attention back and forth between what is left of the tension and the places in your body where you feel relaxed. As you shift from one to the other, note where the tension is lessening and spend time paying attention to the lessening as it moves to other areas in your body.

EMANCIPATE YOURSELF

You might be more accustomed to holding on to what you want than you are to letting go. Our way of life teaches you to possess rather than give, not only with material things but also with feelings. If you get something, you win. If you give up something, you lose. So you're more likely to cling than to let go.

MARCH

CHILL

Surrender is when you're willing to let go of possessive thoughts and feelings and allow yourself to receive. The action of letting go puts you in the most powerful position possible: that of a master instead of a victim. The ability to bend and sway with whatever life sends instead of grabbing on puts you in harmony with it. Then you can surmount the situation, and life runs more smoothly.

See if you can identify a person or event that challenges your ability to let go. The next time you're in the presence of this person or situation, try emancipating yourself. Notice how much freer you feel. Notice how surrender helps reduce anxiety and how fluidity brings you more happiness and peace of mind.

CENTER YOURSELF; DON'T BE SELF-CENTERED

A friend loved the warm, long days of summer. On the longest day of the year, I said to her, "You must be on cloud nine." She replied, "No, I'm sad because tomorrow the days start getting shorter again." When I pointed out that she was shrinking her joy, she was surprised that her narrow viewpoint had hijacked her.

The workaholic mind is a narrow mind without room to grow. It automatically constricts situations and keeps you self-centered without you realizing it. You focus on times when you failed, things that make you hot under the collar, or goals that you haven't accomplished: same lousy job, the usual inconsiderate coworkers, the office party that was nothing to write home about. You build up negativity without realizing it, and that becomes the lens you look through.

The key is to keep a broad perspective, so you don't let pleasantness slip by without savoring it. When you underscore the small things around you (the perfume of a flower or seeing colleagues working as a team) that you appreciate, it fosters a positive slant toward work and personal life, and you feel more joyful inside.

GET SOME SHUT-EYE

It has been said that the best bridge between despair and hope is a good night's sleep. Without sleep, you're at a higher risk of heart disease, and your capacity to learn is compromised. It's important to have regular bedtime hours and make sure the bedroom is cozy, inviting, and well ventilated. It's important to rethink the value of getting plenty of shut-eye. Along with good nutrition and exercise, a good night's sleep doesn't detract from your productivity. On the contrary, it adds to it. When you get ample sleep, you're physically healthier, more productive, and more mentally alert than workers who deprive themselves of this fuel.

MARCH

#CHILL

OBSERVE COMPULSIVE THOUGHTS

If you're like most task masters, although you exceed the expectations of others, you can never reach your own out-of-reach standards. You rely on compulsive thoughts that tell you to take on mountains of additional work—even when your professional and personal lives are overloaded and in disarray. The thoughts stalk you in your sleep, at a party, or while hiking with friends. They beat you to the office before you begin the work-day. They loom over your shoulder during intimate conversations with loved ones. You can't stop thinking about, talking about, or engaging in work tasks. After a while, the addiction becomes an unwelcome burden, but you can't let up because everyone is depending on you.

Try to become mindful of your compulsive thoughts, observing them with curiosity as they stream through your mind. Instead of relying on them, let them come and go without personalizing, resisting, or identifying with them. Eventually they float away.

GO WIDE

When encountering difficulty, try taking a bird's-eye view of the hardship and brainstorm a wide range of possibilities. You can remind yourself that the difficulty isn't a personal failure and that it's not permanent. By looking at the wider view, you can see more possibilities than obstacles. Then you focus on the solution, not the problem. You identify the opportunity contained in each difficulty by asking, "How can I turn this situation around to my favor?" or "Can I find something positive in the downside?" or "How can I put this unfortunate situation in context of the bigger picture?

Scientists call this strategy the broaden-and-build effect as you go wide to weather hard times. When you use this strategy on a regular basis, it has the cumulative effect of making you more optimistic and your driving force the automatic default.

FOCUS ON THE HERE AND NOW

Odds are, if you're like most workaholics, you go through life trying to get the good stuff, and you miss what's happening now. When you start to watch your mind, you become amazed at how it constantly tries to figure out how to maximize pleasure and minimize pain.

You have to get through the traffic jam instead of *being* in the traffic jam. You have to hop in and out of the shower to get to work instead of *being* in the shower. You have to hurry up and get dinner made so you can watch TV instead of *being* present with dinner preparation. As you get lost in fantasies of past

MARCH

#CHILL

or future events, these out-of-the-moment episodes disconnect you from your surroundings and yourself.

To become self-connected, try watching where your mind goes in each moment. You will notice a difference between the times you actually show up and those in which your mind drifts to thoughts of the past or future. Anytime your mind wanders from the present—even as you read these words—simply bring it back to the here and now.

STOP STINKIN' YOUR THINKIN'

What you say to yourself under the duress of work pops up with such lightning speed that you don't even notice. Excessive working is kept alive by exaggerated conclusions you draw, most of which are distorted: "I must be all things to all people or else I'm a failure"; "If I can't do a job right, it's not worth doing"; "I should be loved by everyone."

When you make these kinds of statements, your mind governs by the "alls-or-nones"—the affliction of trying to box life into neat categories. Problem is, life can't be categorized in such an artificial way. "Alls-or-nones" limit possibilities into one extreme or another and undergird all types of addictions. Twelve-Step programs call this mode "stinkin' thinkin'." These exaggerations cloud clarity, limit your choices, and trap you in uncertainty and bad decision making—creating overwork, hampering your relationships, and undermining your personal goals.

If you overestimate your need to work, you probably underestimate how much you actually do work. The next time you get stuck in rigid workaholic thinking, put up your antenna. Listen for self-talk, such as *always, all, everybody,* or *nobody, never, none,* that cues you that the "alls-or-nones" rule. Then focus on the shades of gray and consider flexible possibilities: "I don't have to be all things to all people. My success depends on doing my best."

DON'T KILL TIME

Some people are in such a hurry it seems they want to kill time by working it to death before it kills them. Instead of killing time when caught in rush-hour traffic or long grocery lines, you can accept the moment *exactly* as it is and use it as a shock absorber. Telling yourself that you're choosing to wait empowers instead of victimizes, cushions stress, and cultivates a peaceful, calm spirit. You can harness present moment-centered attention for personal reflection, stretching, or connecting with the rise and fall of your breath.

Instead of getting annoyed at people who move at a snail's pace, think of them as examples of how you

MARCH

#CHILL

can slow down. With a nonjudgmental attitude, you can people-watch and find mirrors of your own impatience and irritability etched on the faces of others.

BEFRIEND YOUR INNER CRITIC

Everybody has an inner critic—that kick-ass voice that lives inside your head, putting you under a microscope. Much like the hard-ass drill sergeant who wants to save his soldiers' lives, the Critic's job is to point out your failures so you don't get your head blown off in combat.

You can't get rid of Critic, so don't even try, but you can develop a relationship with it. Next time Critic blinks in your mind like a neon sign, think of it as a *part* of you, not *all* of you. Listening to it as a separate part, instead of as *you*, gives you distance from it and keeps you from attacking yourself. Once you hear Critic as a part instead of as you, there's room for Confidence— that nurturing and encouraging voice, cheering you on with goodhearted affirmations like a best friend would.

Start giving Confidence equal time, letting it acknowledge your accomplishments and positive qualities. You might imagine Confidence sitting across from you in a chair, as you listen to what it has to say. The more you watch Critic from afar—without getting frustrated or trying to get rid of it—the easier it will be for Confidence to show up and give you a friendly hand.

CULTIVATE EMPATHY

The ability to put yourself in someone else's shoes is a powerful tool. Empathy connects you to others and frees you from narrow, negative thinking and snap judgments. It enables you to feel the pain someone else goes through and neutralizes hard feelings. It imbues you with patience, calmness, and compassion to deal with difficult people to settle disputes or keep calm when someone explodes.

This approach works in your best interests because empathy makes you a kinder, more loving person. It shows you a bigger perspective so you can respond in a way that promotes fairness and good communication. And when you're in the office, putting yourself in the place of a disgruntled client or coworker can diffuse tension-charged situations.

Suppose you stand in the shoes of someone who upset you. Imagine walking around inside that person's body, looking at the upsetting event while in their skin, through their eyes, with their heart. As you consider the angles others take in situations, your hard feelings soften, you feel liberated from your narrow, negative thinking, and you can chill.

MARCH

#CHILL

PRIORITIZE

If you're walking the tightrope of work/life balance, each day you have a swirl of tasks to complete. Some have to do with your job. Perhaps others relate to family and personal commitments and some are more essential than others. It's important for you to decide which ones come first and to have clear, practical priorities. As you plan out the days ahead, don't prioritize work tasks first. Group all the tasks based on each sphere of your life: personal, work, family, and play. Within each grouping, decide which tasks are most urgent.

To cultivate work/life balance and prevent you from prioritizing all the work items as most important, you prioritize a minimum of one priority per life sphere. This strategy encourages you to include each of your life's spheres. Then you tackle the most important ones first in each sphere. You put nonessentials on the back burner or farm them out to someone else if possible. When you reflect back on your priorities, you can ensure that you complete each priority in each of the spheres of your life.

FORGET YOUR FREE PASS

Many of us give more tender loving care to our jobs than to our families. Though we don't party, waste time, or spend egregiously, we don't always show up for the people we love when we need to.

No matter how much money you make or how hard you work, you don't get a free pass for not being accountable to your personal life. It's not okay to be content with being a lousy parent or spouse. It's insensitive, arrogant, and disrespectful to treat loved ones as if they're business appendages and drag them wherever you want. In recovery from overworking, inventory your intimate relationships. Do you treat loved ones humanely? Are you respectful of their time and emotional needs? What hurtful habits do you need to amend to be a more loving human being?

DODGE DECISION FATIGUE

Studies show that a decision-fatigued brain becomes worn out from hours of nonstop working, depleted of its mental energy for making decisions outside of work. Basically, the more choices you make in extended hours, the harder it is for your strained mind to make even the simplest decision: what to wear, where to eat, how much to spend, or how to prioritize work projects.

But life doesn't wait for you. Your loved ones and coworkers depend on you. You take shortcuts, make impulsive work decisions, and gobble junk food. You

MARCH

#CHILL

defer household preferences to family members, failing to show up for important life decisions. You can remedy this situation by devoting to your brain the same restorative rest your body needs throughout the day: brisk exercise, power napping, meditation, stretching, deep breathing, contemplating nature, yoga, or tai chi.

CREATE VISUAL REST

Chances are you spend an inordinate amount of time bound to your desk. Windowless cubicles and airless open-floor plans can take a toll on job performance. It's no longer debatable that the great outdoors gives strength to body and soul. Studies show that natural elements such as plants, light, or blue, green, and yellow colors found in nature benefit productivity, creativity, and overall mental health.

If you can't get outdoors for a break, evaluate your personal workstation for environmental stressors you might not be aware of. Then see what simple steps you can take to create visual rest. If you don't have a window, bring in nature photos, green plants, a table-top waterfall that makes calming bubbling sounds, a fish bowl, or a terrarium. And let Mother Nature quiet your mind and relax the frantic pandemonium of work demands.

RECLAIM YOUR CHILDHOOD

What does work addiction have to do with your upbringing? Everything. The first time I spoke with Gloria Steinem, we both said, "I feel like I know you." Although our lives were different on the outside, the way we experienced them was much the same. We shared an emotional blueprint: isolation, pain, loss, fear, and sometimes embarrassment. Comrades of the soul bound together by common childhood wounds, we both became self-professed workaholics to deal with our childhood struggles.

Many workaholics grow up in unstable families, forced to forfeit a carefree childhood and assume grown-up emotional burdens bigger than they can bear. If this is you, you become a serious little adult and forget how to play. Your job is to stabilize your family, latching on to anything predictable and consistent—an anchor to keep you afloat amid the instability.

You seek control through housework or homework. Once grown, your nervous system stays on red alert. Who wants to be in the present moment when past-present moments were so unpleasant? Your mind automatically seeks an escape hatch into sources of pleasure and safety: tasks and caretaking. In recovery you find that sweet spot where job success and personal fulfillment reside side by side.

MARCH

#CHILL

BE POSITIVE

When you're under the gun with looming deadlines or overloaded with work tasks, the mind is designed to constrict and target the negative threat. When you're searching for a solution to a work crisis, negativity keeps you mired in the problem. To say you're not going to worry, that you're just going to be happy, doesn't do justice to the scientific underpinnings of positivity's depth and power as an antidote to work addiction.

Positivity isn't drinking some magical joy juice, wearing rose-colored glasses, or putting your head in the sand. It's taking realistic, constructive steps to deal with life instead of succumbing to it. Positivity stretches your mind open to take in as much information as you can and widens the array of possibilities. While negativity keeps you focused on the problem, a positive approach allows you to focus on a workable solution.

You can practice looking for the silver lining in situations you label as negative. You can get in the habit of looking at the big picture. When things are stormy, you can find one or two positive things you enjoy or look forward to. You can surround yourself with positive thinkers and let their optimistic mojo rub off on you.

EVALUATE THE STORIES YOU TELL

What stories do you tell yourself about your work and balance? Are there narratives too difficult to face? Which ones did you varnish, edit, or deny? And which ones did you bury deep within or forget until they rose up and ignited your hard-driving work style?

Even if you don't share your stories with others you still have a particular way of justifying what you do. Perhaps you say, "I don't work that much" or "I work a lot to support my family" or "It's the type of job I'm in; I don't have a choice." Your stories are not objective accounts of reality. You often have a way of telling your stories to make you look like a hero and those who confront you look like villains. The story, how often you tell it, to whom you tell it, and in what way you tell it dramatically affects your life. Your story might glorify you, promote your accomplishments, or show how well you handle difficult situations.

As you address work/life balance, you can learn to make your story accurate and objective. That requires considering the different stories carried by the ones who love you and work alongside you. You question whether you're caught telling a story that blames others or whether it portrays you taking responsibility for your part.

MARCH

ACCEPT YOUR LIMITATIONS

Self-victimization, negativity, and self-pity become habitual ways of thinking. These limitations manifest in the chronic patterns of living in which some people find themselves: jobless, alone, bored, miserable. The prison bars are the old judgments, fears, and worries that you erect from past hurts and fears, recycled through the present.

Once you understand that it's your limited view that prevents your life from working, not the reality of the world, everything changes for the better. How can you cut down on the self-pitying attitude? How else can you change your attitude to accept and move past limitations?

RECOGNIZE YOU'RE GOOD ENOUGH

At what point do you ever say, "That's good enough"? Perhaps through your eyes, such an idea is a mirage. But you keep looking for it like the seahorse looking for the sea because he can't see the water he's swimming in, so he spends his life searching for what he already has.

You work through holidays, miss your kids' events, or pull all-nighters—all in attempts to be good enough. But no matter how hard you try, you tell yourself that nothing is quite good enough. That message of failure fills you with shame and self-contempt. To medicate the bad feelings, you dig your heels in deeper and try to excel even more.

Is this the way you want to continue to live? What if you center yourself and become mindful of what you're doing? What if you drop the illusion that some work task will make you feel good enough? Welcome self-compassion and allow it to overtake you, knowing that everything is possible and everything is unknown until you start to live it.

SURRENDER

Step 3 of Workaholics Anonymous says, you turn over your self-will to sources outside yourself for help: the support of a Twelve-Step group, insight during an inspirational reading, a Higher Power, or a sudden realization when listening to a sponsor. Through these simple acts, you relinquish your omnipotence, realize you don't have all the answers, and stand face-to-face on the same level with others in a common spirit. In other words, you put your ego on the back burner.

Your ability to surrender control over excessive work habits carries over into other aspects of your

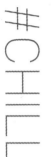

life. You discover that controlling other people and situations creates stress and frustration. Putting this admission into daily practice on the job, at home, and in social situations paradoxically frees you of addictive patterns, cultivates positive relationships, and fills the empty void.

MARCH TAKEAWAYS

- Put on your wide-angle lens and look at the big picture of your life to reveal the blind spots that your zoom lens clouds out.

- Befriend your inner critic and seek to understand how it is trying to protect you from life's curveballs.

- Offset decision fatigue with the trifecta of stress reduction: restorative rest and sleep, healthy eating, and regular exercise.

- Avoid being a desk potato by bringing the great outdoors inside periodically and immersing yourself in Mother Nature's healing effects.

- Be able to see that letting go and surrendering—the opposite of giving up or giving in—are actions of personal strength, not defeat.

APRIL

If you want to be
respected by others,
the great thing is to
respect yourself.
Only by that, only by
self-respect will you
compel others to
respect you.

—FYODOR DOSTOEVSKY

OPEN-MINDED AWARENESS

April, the fourth month of the year, is derived from the Latin *aperire*, "to open," referring to the time of the year when flowers and trees open, baby birds hatch, and spring awakens. In the same vein, the fourth month is a time to make a fearless moral inventory of yourself. As you open your mind to closer self-examination, you gain an awareness of how you lost yourself in busyness. Without judgment, you identify your strengths and limitations so you're more conscious of the traits that are conducive to or impeding your growth.

You take full responsibility for your inability to chill instead of blaming it on a bitter conflict at work, family pressures, or the head honchos who ditched your creative idea. You start to see more clearly and honestly your ill temperedness, self-righteousness, and judgmental attitude, and you're able to admit them to yourself without self-condemnation.

In this chapter, you have a chance to chill with open-mindedness as you cultivate work/life integration: attunement of body, mind, and spirit. You make a mindful reciprocal connection with your breath to anchor you in the present moment and lift your spirits and productivity. You become harmonious with

CHILL

the imperfection of the world and the acceptance of *all* that life sends your way. You realize everything isn't an emergency, and that, in fact, few things are as urgent as you make them. You open yourself more to life's own rhythm and flow, accept life on its own terms, and synchronize with its rhythm, putting yourself in unison with it. You are reminded there are only twenty-four hours in a day.

During this month, you ask what actions you can take to open yourself to a full life. Perhaps open yourself to opposing views? Leave old ruts and routines and face new challenges? Change unhealthy work habits? Take a different approach that stretches you out of your comfort zone? Or form new relationships or deepen intimacy with old ones?

LEARN TO CONNECT WITH YOUR BREATH

A mindful connection with your breath anchors you in the place where true life occurs moment to moment. Try this meditation exercise for five minutes. Sit in a comfortable place with eyes closed. Breathing in through your nose and out through the mouth, focus on each inhalation and exhalation. Follow your breath through to a full cycle from the beginning when the lungs are full back down to when they're empty. Then start all over again.

As you stay with this cycle, mindfully watching your breath, thoughts usually arise in the form of judgment: wondering if you're doing it right, thinking about tasks you have to do later, debating if it's worth your time. Don't try to get rid of your thoughts. Allow them to arise and accept whatever arises with openhearted-ness, bringing your attention gently back and focusing on the breath.

Each time your attention strays from the breath (and it will), bring your awareness back to it. There's nowhere else to be, nothing else to do but notice your breath. If your mind gets caught in a chain of thoughts, gently step out of the thought stream and come back to the sensations of your breath. After five minutes or more, open your eyes and notice how much more connected you are to the present moment.

DECLUTTER

One of the best ways "to open" on the physical plane is to declutter and cleanse your physical environ-ment. On top of your workaholic pace, disorganized and cluttered living spaces make your life even more chaotic and stressful. Clutter is a roadblock to find-

APRIL

CHILL

ing things you need. It cuts into valuable time and adds another level of frustration when you're already in a hurry. As clutter piles up, your stress level can go sky-high. You might find your productivity wanes, too, as you bounce from one task to another, paralyzed by where to begin.

After a long day, the last thing you want is a stressful visual reminder of what needs doing staring you in the face. You can create visual rest by decluttering—deciding what you need and what you don't. Then organize the keepers and toss, recycle, or donate anything you haven't used in more than a year. You might also consider digitizing paperwork to declutter your paper trail. Signing up for online billing and payments eliminates excess mail, checks, and paper clutter.

Sometimes when you hang on to junk on the physical plane, you harbor something inside that clogs your productivity or blocks creative flow. Once you declutter and organize your physical environment, you often notice a parallel process on the psychological level. You start to notice an unclogging of old ideas, toxic relationships, and bad habits, along with more room for inspiration, clarity, and creativity.

BE MINDFUL OF YOUR BLIND SPOTS

Perfection goes against the grain of the imperfection of which the universe is made. In its clutches, perfection tightens its stranglehold on you, injects rigidity into your bloodstream, and chokes the flow of spontaneous and flexible ideas.

Uncurbed, the desire for perfection causes you to set unrealistic goals, overdo it, and overfocus on your mistakes. This distorted perspective creates blind spots that prevent you from seeing how awesome you already are and how often you get it right. The result is feelings of inadequacy, which trigger more work perfection toward unreachable ideals, which leads to self-defeat and back to where you started: inadequacy.

It's time you start telling yourself the truth. There's no such thing as perfection. Nobody can attain it. You can set high standards that are possible to reach without putting yourself under intolerable conditions that create endless work hours, stress, fatigue, and physical illness. What are you prepared to do to put yourself in unison with the imperfection of the world?

DE-STRESS

Most things are not an emergency. Urgency is not a product of work or life. It's a by-product of your inabil-

#CHILL

ity to take life on life's terms. You don't wait around for stress to slug you. You thrive on it, get revved up, and bring it on yourself. Nothing moves fast enough. When a job is left hanging, you feel anxious. You over-schedule and constantly rush against the clock. Then you start to resent the commitments you made.

The problem is that stress is more powerful than you. It loves a good fight, and it always wins. When you constantly pressure yourself, you suffer in body, mind, and spirit. When you're frazzled, the brain acts as an internal slingshot, pumping a cocktail of stress hormones into your bloodstream. The chest heaves, heart rate jumps, blood pressure leaps, respiration rate skyrockets, and muscles tighten, readying you for action. The brain tells your body to stay in this alert state until it's convinced the threat is over.

Stress makes you believe that everything must happen right now. Stop trying to match the breakneck speed of light and step out of the stress rut. Because you created the urgency in the first place, you can stop biting off more than you can chew.

QUIT *KAROSHI*'ING

The Japanese coined a name for their ten thousand workers a year who drop dead from putting in sixty-to-seventy-hour workweeks: *karoshi*—which translates as death from overwork. Otherwise healthy workers keel over at their desks after a long stretch of overtime or after consummating a high-pressure deal, usually from a stroke or heart attack. *Karoshi* among corporate workers in their forties and fifties is so common that the Japanese workplace has been dubbed "a killing field." In India work addiction is called "a poison by slow motion."

Although we don't have comparable English names for *karoshi*, corporate breadwinners dropping dead from overwork have been making headlines for decades in the United States. Workers who labor fifty-five-hour weeks are a third more likely to suffer a stroke than those working fewer than forty hours.

You can take a personal inventory of your work hours and overtime you invest in your job. One thing to ask yourself is, do you have time away from work to recharge your batteries? Do you have a hobby, a favorite pastime, or a spiritual practice that absorbs stress and gives you a chance to refuel with energy?

DO NOTHING

The mantra for recovering workaholics is "Don't just do something—sit there." I can imagine you rolling your eyes, glancing at your to-do list, wondering if I've been sniffing the ink cartridge from my computer.

APRIL

#CHILL

I realize the idea of doing nothing is a bitter pill to swallow. When you slow down and watch the grass grow, you start to go through withdrawal. You fidget, become restless and agitated. Maybe you snap at people around you. The only solution seems to be to get up and start doing something.

But the art of doing nothing is good medicine. It gives your mind and body a chance to go through a withdrawal period until you come out the other side more chilled. In those moments of withdrawal that might seem empty and needless, what has been there all along in some embryonic form is given space and comes to life. The Italians call it *il dolce far niente*—roughly translated as "the sweetness of doing nothing." Doing nothing is like the pauses that are integral to a beautiful piece of music. Without absences of sound, music would be just noise. Doing nothing provides an incubation period for your work ideas to hatch and feelings for loved ones to thaw.

STOP BELIEVING EVERYTHING YOU THINK

Workaholics have an incessant stream of negative thoughts that drive their addiction. When you believe the chatter in your mind's echo chamber, it becomes a reality. If you believe the thought that you're unworthy, unlovable, ugly—even though others may not perceive you that way—your impression that "I'm an undeserving person" is still a fact inside your mind.

If you're like most people, you don't behave on the basis of objective reality but on the basis of what you perceive to be true, whether your perceptions match objective reality or are illusions. Albert Einstein called it "an optical illusion of consciousness."

You believe the thought streams running through your mind at the time. But you can bring an awareness of the incessant mind streams by watching them with curiosity without self-judgment or believing they're true. A dispassionate eye helps you become more aware of how the mind's chatter can make you feel miserable. Once you develop this mindfulness, you learn not to believe everything you think and to reduce your suffering.

AVOID AVOIDANCE

It's hard. It's messy. And it's liberating. But can you face conflict at home or in the workplace? Gulp! Odds are you're averse to conflict, and you immerse yourself into work to escape from facing it. Avoiding conflict gives you temporary relief from the stress of coping with an uncomfortable situation, but it doesn't go away; it simply festers and becomes worse until it eventually explodes.

APRIL

When you avoid conflict because you're afraid of facing someone's anger, it can appear from the outside that you're hiding something. Adding insult to injury, you're left with a double whammy to deal with the conflict you initially avoided plus others' suspicion of deceit and trust issues.

Conflict avoidance is a form of running for the hills when tension builds. It prevents you from getting that job promotion, cultivating a deeper intimate relationship, or strengthening your resilience. If you want to live fully, your serenity takes priority over avoidance. You take a deep breath, muster your courage, and face the music. Usually you discover that the thing you're most afraid of facing is the very thing that can set you free.

GRASP AT GREAT SHADOWS

Does routine run your life? Have you ever broken with petty reality, taken a great risk and found it to be life altering: lucrative investments, rich friendships, adventure, and fun-filled times?

You need rules, routines, and schedules. You need them to keep your life in order, but how many wonderful experiences and people have you excluded by living your life by the book? Sometimes you unknowingly limit your work/life balance out of fear of embracing something new and unknown. Perhaps you do this from a need for security and predictability. You frequent the same restaurant, hold the same job, follow the same daily routine, and stay in the same close-knit circle of friends. Perhaps holding on to the familiar feels comfortable, but it restricts you.

You can break these boring, humdrum habits and eliminate sameness by welcoming change into some area of your life. You can get out of straitjacketed daily routines, even if it's as simple as taking a different route home from work, going to a new restaurant, or taking a different approach in building a successful relationship. You can welcome opposing views, knowing that other people's ways might be different from your own but valid nonetheless. Perhaps the key to a more integrated, balanced, and chilled life lies in the shadows you have avoided.

DARE TO ADVENTURE

If you look at your life from a bird's-eye view, what would you see? Dread of another pressure-cooker day? Or exciting challenges that lie ahead? Would you push through the minutes with your head stuck in newspapers, smartphones, and email? Or would you begin to look at people as intriguing, engaging them in conversation and showing renewed interest in what

APRIL

#CHILL

they have to say? Would you snap at loved ones or try to be more patient with their human fallibilities without trying to change them?

When you think you've seen and done it all, these are only habitual thoughts that you can change. You have the power to change your daily grind simply by the view you take of it. If you live each day with an open heart, as a first-time experience, something magical happens. Life takes on a shimmering glow. You have a renewed outlook, a deeper appreciation for yourself, and a richer satisfaction out of life. You feel compassion for others, perhaps those you ignored or took for granted. You gain respect for coworkers and your job. Learn to rediscover each new day as a song to sing and an adventure to dare instead of a grind to endure.

DON'T "MUSTURBATE"

Most overachievers have a disease that psychologist Albert Ellis coined "musturbation"—bowing to the demands of others, the world, and the negative self-talk. If you suffer from this malady, your work and personal life are ruled by oppositional terms such as *should, ought, must,* and *have to.*

"I must win that contract"; "I must get that promotion"; "My family must do what I say"; "Others must see my point of view"; "Life must be easier than this." These self-imposed mandatory rules have a powerful effect on your outlook, feelings, and actions. Musturbation gives rise to frustration, anger, and depression. And it drives your overdoing when inevitably the world and other people don't conform to your "musterbatory rules."

By asking if your self-talk is compassionate or oppressive, you become more aware of what you require of yourself and choose more supportive, comforting words: "I can do my best to win that contract" or "Although life won't always be easy, I can still meet its challenges." Replacing mandatory statements with empowering words puts you more in charge instead of at the mercy of situations. And it enhances your well-being.

DETHRONE THE INNER BULLY

If you're like most task masters, you have an inner bully that runs your life. It kicks you around and keeps you focused on your flaws so you constantly feel as if you're struggling. The workaholic's solution? Work longer and harder. Yet immersing yourself in tasks mires you deeper into the problem. That's why it's called work addiction. Of course, that's not the real solution.

APRIL

#CHILL

The real solution is to develop more self-kindness to chill your self-judgment. And that solution is backed up by studies that show encouragement and self-support are game changers. The more self-compassion you have, the greater your emotional arsenal and the higher your job performance and ability to maintain work/life balance.

Self-compassion limits the distress that leads to self-castigation. Chilled workers can admit their mistakes without self-condemnation. Where do you stand? When your inner bully kicks you when you're down, amp up your kind, compassionate side, pick yourself up, and brush yourself off. As you hop back in the saddle, forgive and support yourself with encouragement and lovingkindness.

WORK "AS IF"

Raise your hand if nonstop working has hampered your ability to express feelings, if you're stumped on how to feel in emotional situations, or if you'd like to feel more intimacy but don't know how. I thought so. Chances are you have overworked for a long period of time and gotten stuck in one way or another somewhere along the way. But there's good news. Twelve-Step programs have bandied about a phrase for years called "acting as if." This principle can help you get through periods of emotional paralysis.

What does it mean to act as if? It is a simple yet powerful tool that says you can create outer circumstances by acting as if they're already true. You give a certain performance as if it's how you feel. The mood you pretend becomes a reality. Suppose you're angry and unforgiving but want to be forgiving toward someone who offends you. You can come to feel forgiving by acting as if you *are* forgiving. Perhaps you are cold and detached but want to be happy for a coworker's promotion. You can act as if you *are* happy—and find you are. Maybe you're worried about a huge deadline, but you convince yourself it's easy and tackle the difficulty with enthusiasm instead of dread. When you tell yourself that a challenge is a piece of cake, you might be surprised at how easy an obstacle becomes a cinch to work through.

BEFRIEND WORRY

Worry goes ahead of you like a scouting party before challenging situations. It stalks you before a big day at work and lurks over your shoulder when you're pitching ideas. The anchor of worry weighs you down and robs you of strength. Even when things go well,

APRIL

CHILL

you wait for the ax to fall. Worry during both calm *and* troubled times creates a 24/7, worry-filled life. Living this way creates wear and tear on your mind and body.

If you think of worry as an infiltrating enemy and try to extinguish it, you create an adversarial relationship, which leads to more internal frustration, anxiety, and chaos. It's counterintuitive, but the key is to forge a new relationship with worry by welcoming and befriending it. Even though you perceive worry to be working against you, it's actually on your side—a protector, warning of a threat, trying to keep you out of harm's way. The more you are able to think of worry as your friend, instead of your enemy, the less worry and more chill time you will have.

ACCEPT A COSMIC SLAP

A seismic event can rattle the foundation of your understanding of life and your place in it. But what matters is what you do with it. In his book *The Art of Happiness,* the Dalai Lama tells of a woman who prospered from a financial windfall after a profitable business investment. Her sudden, meteoric success gave her lots of money, free time, and retirement at a young age. After the dust settled, things returned to normal, and the woman said she was no happier than before the windfall.

He contrasts her situation to a man who contracted HIV. Devastated at the news, he spent a year getting over the shock and disbelief. But taking the opportunity to explore spirituality for the first time, he found his life transformed in positive ways. He got more out of each day than ever before and strangely felt happier than before the diagnosis.

Material gain—a new house, car, or money—can bring temporary highs that flatten out after a short period of time. Tragedy or loss can plummet you to an all-time low for a while. But eventually your mood rises back to normal. Regardless of whether life throws you highs or lows, the important thing is what you do with the seismic events in it. You have the power to create how you experience that life. No matter how painful or difficult, big or small, turn each experience around with openhearted acceptance and make it an opportunity to grow.

RULE WITH A SOFTER HAND

Hard-hitting workers tend to rule with an iron fist: their way or the highway. While alcoholics like nothing better than a drinking buddy, if you're a workaholic, you probably prefer a working buddy who matches your own inhuman standards of long hours and frantic pace. In the workplace, you have contempt for slack-

APRIL

#CHILL

ers and use pressure and intimidation as a defense against your own securities, undermining—rather than supporting—colleagues or subordinates to reinforce your own powerful position.

If you're a workaholic boss with autocratic control, under your leadership employee morale nosedives and burnout skyrockets. You push and hurry subordinates to the point that they feel undue stress. And you're probably out of touch with your employees' emotional lives and insensitive to their needs and feelings.

American corporations have discovered that the healthiest work environments are those that consider human factors and nurture their employees. If you're a manager who provides a healthy role model and inspires through nudging instead of force, the company will achieve more creative productivity, higher revenues, and a more balanced workforce.

CHECK YOUR TRANSMISSION

Work addiction isn't contagious, but it has damaging effects that are transmitted to those who live with us. Children of workaholics have higher depression and anxiety levels and believe circumstantial events control their lives. They carry these psychological scars well into adulthood, when they rely on others for decision making, have more incidences of obsessive-compulsive behaviors, and lack confidence associated with greater anxiety and depression than the population at large.

Many children of workaholics pick up the message that they can't measure up or that something is wrong with them because they're valued for their performance, not for who they are. With parental expectations out of reach, they internalize failure as their own inadequacy. Many end up addicted to work and performance themselves.

On your deathbed you wouldn't wish you'd spent more time working and less time with your family. Since tomorrow holds no guarantees, perhaps it's time to take action before you have irreversible regrets. You might make a dinner date to meet with your sons and daughters, initiate long walks and heart-to-heart talks, or plan special activities or trips to repair the broken bonds. Listen to what they have to say, find out what they've been up to, and let them know how much they mean to you.

DECOMPRESS

What if you harnessed the pressure from job demands to promote work/life balance? What if you required yourself to spend an equal amount of time with loved

APRIL

CHILL

ones as you spend working? What if corporate managers said you had to take an equal amount of time off every time you call the office or check emails on a holiday? What if you had to take on-site meditation classes in the workplace proportionate to the number of sales you make? What if businesses required you to take holidays and vacations without working? What if you approached family mealtimes, anniversaries, and reunions with the same motivation you approach work deadlines? What if you pressured yourself to get to your kids' events as much as you do to get to work on time? What if you scheduled as many fun times with family and friends as you do meetings with coworkers?

Just imagine what a wonderful world it would be if you had fewer headaches, digestive problems, or chest pain. And you had less worry and more joy, less stress and more peace of mind, and less hurry and more chill. Imagine what it would be like if you slowed the moment down and enjoyed it.

BE KIND TO THE EARTH

Take an opportunity to reflect on your part in your small corner of the planet to make a positive impact on the world so that it resonates with more joy and love.

Think about cleaning up your act and being kinder to the planet you live on. Ask yourself what you can do to be more environmentally friendly and save the planet for those who come after you: reduce your carbon footprint, recycle, and go paperless. You can walk more softly, move more slowly, and take more peaceful steps on the earth during your workday. When your mind drifts to the past or future, you can ground yourself in the present moment to work for the cause of peace and happiness for all of humanity.

Astronaut Peggy Whitson spent more time in space than any other American. Seeing the entire earth from her perch prompted her to remark, "We need to do more to be one earth, one people." Ask what part you can play on Earth Day to practice work/life balance. The more you clean your side of the street by slowing your pace and creating more joy, the more you contribute to greater balance on the planet.

GO HIGH WHEN THEY GO LOW

When a coworker or supervisor betrays you, how do you respond? Do you harbor resentment because it gives you emotional satisfaction? That's like eating rat poison and waiting for the rat to die. Sustained resentment works against you and blocks your passion and

#CHILL

productivity. It keeps anger and hurt at the center of your workday, depletes your energy, and focuses you in a negative direction.

From the backstabbing coworker to the distrusting boss, to the meddling in-law, you're in charge of how you respond to the people in your life. Those who anger you conquer you. It's up to you to decide whether you're conquered or strengthened by backstabbers. You can give someone else's negativity power over your life or focus on what's important for your own happiness. When backstabbers go low, you go high and reap the benefits of a positive direction at work, home, and play.

HOLD THE LINE

When spouses and children of workaholics complain, they get blank looks from those around them. Business consultants and clinicians alike often suggest that families simply accept and adapt to the workaholic's schedule or tell spouses to stop complaining. Family members are told to center their lives around the workaholic's schedule, join in the addiction by taking children to the workplace, and anticipate spending a lot of time alone.

In the mental health world, the buzzword *integration* refers to enabling or blurred boundaries, and it creates family dysfunction. Studies show that flexible work boundaries often turn into work *without* boundaries. And just the expectation of checking emails after hours can be hazardous to your health.

Taking children on a business trip or to the office once in a while shows kids what parents do when they're not home with them. But integrating spouses and children into the work world on a regular basis keeps work addiction at the center of family life and inadvertently overshadows the lives of other family members. Although Silicon Valley admires this sort of "dedication" to work, it's an example of how many big businesses enable work addiction and contribute to the demise of family cohesion and stability.

In recovery, you develop clarity to distinguish between blurred boundaries and healthy lines. Work is a separate part of your life, not all of it. And you earn an A-plus for not letting work bleed into personal moments with your loved ones.

DELEGATE

If you're having trouble turning a project over to someone else, you can learn to delegate in order to perform optimally. Of course, if you're a workaholic that's easier said than done. Beneath the inability to delegate is a fear that something is being taken from

APRIL

#CHILL

you, the fear of loss of control over the outcome. Even if you pass along a project, you're apt to be compelled to breathe down the neck of the person who assumes responsibility for it. Maybe you're afraid to let it go because you believe no one else can handle it as well as you. You'll work days and nights on end to make sure it's done right instead of wasting time with a bunch of bad ideas from coworkers.

It's important to reframe the art of delegating. You don't think of it as passing off work you don't want to do. And you don't fear that delegating tasks or asking for help is perceived as a sign of weakness or incompetence. You don't look at it as sacrificing the quality of a project, either. You look at delegating as an opportunity to stretch and improve yourself—to be a creative collaborator and good team player. As you learn to let go, you encourage coworkers to stretch their skills and judgment. And ultimately, by sharing the workload, you unburden yourself.

ACCEPT UNCERTAINTY

At first glance that does seem like a pretty tall order. Life is full of unexpected curveballs. If uncertainty is unacceptable to you, it turns into fear, and you fight it tooth and nail, creating more tension.

Expectations about persuading the boss to see your point of view or to take a course of action for the company can lead you to wrap your thoughts and feelings around the outcome, setting yourself up for disappointment and resentment. You use a lot of energy getting upset over things you can't control instead of doing the best you can and welcoming uncertainty with open arms.

Truth be told, uncertainty is certain; it's one of the few things we can count on. Your ability to accept it beforehand cultivates peace of mind. In the words of writer Eckhart Tolle, "If uncertainty is perfectly acceptable, it turns into increased aliveness, alertness, and creativity."

Ask yourself if you've resisted uncertain situations and then noticed the tension in your body that accompanied the resistance. Fully surrendering to uncertainty reduces frustration and anxiety and creates an open heart, peaceful presence, and clear mind.

CULTIVATE FRIENDSHIPS

Your friendships are reflections of how secure you are on the inside. You must feel safe enough to let friends see you without your mask and agree to love them unconditionally, too, when they reveal themselves to

APRIL

you—warts and all. Despite their fallibilities, you're able to love them enough to want to create a two-way relationship.

Do you have one person with whom you share this type of bond? If you don't have a close friendship, you have to want it badly enough to stick your neck out. You must be willing to reveal what disturbs you, to share what you're afraid of, to risk letting others see the most vulnerable parts, and to share what you've been unable to discuss.

EMBRACE BROKENNESS

Life breaks everyone to some degree, and if you've lived for a length of time, you're broken in some way. Afterward, you're stronger in those broken places. Since the beginning of time, philosophers, novelists, and songwriters have popularized the notion that what doesn't kill you makes you stronger.

The last thing you want to hear when you're struggling uphill is that the pain makes you stronger. If you're like most people, you harbor wounds lodged in your heart and soul—wounds that inspire an attitude of resilience and determination. Learning from difficult experiences enables you to grow stronger each time you pick yourself up one more time than you fall.

You can turn a negative experience into a positive one, failure into success, a setback into forward movement. The power residing in your broken places is stronger than the challenges that lie before you. You wouldn't be whole if you didn't embrace your brokenness as an integral part of your life. In the words of the Holocaust survivor and psychologist Viktor Frankl, "The way in which a man accepts his fate and all the suffering it entails, the way in which he takes up his cross, gives him ample opportunity—even under the most difficult circumstances—to add a deeper meaning to his life."

EXAMINE YOURSELF

Step 4 of Workaholics Anonymous recommends making a searching and fearless moral inventory of yourself. This self-examination helps you pinpoint your strengths and limitations so you can identity the traits conducive to or impeding your growth and the growth of others.

You might identify your inability to delegate work tasks to subordinates or peers, knowing deep down that coworkers can perform as well or better than you. You might realize your standards are unrealistic and unfair to those with whom you work, live, and

APRIL

#CHILL

play. Or perhaps you examine your intolerance and impatience with people who don't keep the same pace or rigid adherence to your ways and viewpoints. Are you open-minded about an uncertain future or career outcome? Or have you crossed your arms, planted your feet, and made up your mind? After examining what points of view, potential experiences, or possible friendships you've closed out of your life, ask, "What can I open up to more in order to enrich my life and grow as a fulfilled human being?"

APRIL TAKEAWAYS

- Make a fearless inventory of your work/life integration and identify the strengths and limitations that are conducive to or impeding your growth, joy, and serenity.

- Practice mindful breathing to anchor you in the present moment.

- Remember that everything isn't an emergency and put your goals and activities in unison with life instead of trying to put life in unison with your own agenda.

- Practice the art of doing nothing once in a while.

- Delegate.

- Make peace with worry and your inner bully.

- Don't believe everything you think.

MAY

To grow fully as a person, seek out challenging situations that help you bloom instead of safe situations that wither you on the vine.

ADMITTING YOUR FUCKUPS

The month of May is named after Maia, the Roman goddess of growth and productivity. It is helpful to think of this month as a time of personal growth—a time to cultivate honesty and integrity in order to prosper. Studies show you are more likely to fulfill your potential by cultivating a growth mindset—the view that struggles, mistakes, and challenges are part of a learning process, not defeat, that make you smarter, more successful, and happier.

If you were to plot your personal growth on a scale, it would make an upward zigzag, not follow an ascending straight line. A setback is part of your growth process as long as you own up to it, learn from it, and correct it. Problem is, your entire identity is wrapped up in being perfect and competent in everything you do. You admit you got accepted at Yale but conceal that you were rejected at Harvard. You can't bear to be viewed as being wrong or making mistakes. You try to avoid them, cover them up, or pretend they didn't happen. If someone brings the mistake to your attention, you become defensive and deny or justify your wrong-doing. Your credibility and integrity are on the hook, and concealing the mistake becomes a bigger failure than the original fuckup.

CHILL

In this chapter, you develop a heightened ability to act from confidence and chill after a fuckup. The hitch? Admitting it. This month is a time to face your denial, self-deception, and rationalization and give more oxygen to personal growth. When you conceal or deny wrongdoing, you put the problem at the forefront of your future. In the short term, it might seem easier to hide a mistake and pretend it didn't happen. But when you make yourself vulnerable and confide in someone the exact nature of your missteps (for example, people you neglected and hurt because of your bad work habits or denial that walled you off from truth and integrity), you put the problem behind you. As a result of this action, the unburdening of your shame, self-hatred, and isolation dares you to do things differently, to change work-addictive habits, and to live more fully.

When you accept your human fallibility, you experience a new attitude toward life. You discover daily practices that bring more work resiliency, relationship intimacy, and work/life integration. You find tips to deal with job stress, imbalanced work habits, and prolonged sitting during work jags. And you learn the importance of prioritizing self-care, contemplation, and self-reflection and developing safe and meaningful ways to connect with others outside work. You enjoy your job more and find ways to complete tasks more honestly and effectively. You put work in its proper place and have more time for yourself, relationships, and fun. You continue to risk making mistakes, admit the nature of your fuckups, and use them as an opportunity to grow.

CHANT

Chanting has been a practice all over the world for thousands of years, from Native Americans to Gregorian monks. Of all the spiritual practices in which I've engaged, chanting is one of the most satisfying, calming traditions to relax the mind and body from stress.

The physical act of breathing and forming sounds brings body and mind together in a fun and creative way. There are many ways to chant. One of the most common is to simply chant "Om," considered by Hindus to be the universal vibration that exists within every word. There are also many CDs that contain a variety of different chants that you can follow.

To start, I recommend you chant for only five or ten minutes, gradually increasing your sit time to twenty or thirty minutes. Once you find a comfortable, quiet

MAY

place, take a deep breath and relax your body. You can close your eyes or leave them open or half-open. You can chant aloud or silently. Breathing normally, repeat "Om" in a slow, rhythmic way as you exhale. Instead of chanting with every exhalation, you can chant "Om," take a breath or two, and then chant again. Draw the sound from your navel, allowing the sound vibration to rise upward with your breath slowly until it resonates in your nostrils.

GET MOVING!

I admit it: working out sucks. But let's look at the alternative. Most Americans spend an average of ten hours a day in a car, at a desk, or in front of a screen. Your body wasn't designed to sit for long periods of time, and doing so can lower your life expectancy and put you at an 80 percent greater risk of dying from cardiovascular disease.

Experts know that regular exercise builds resistance to stress, increases blood flow and oxygen throughout the body, lowers blood pressure, and improves overall mental and physical health. When you get moving, physical tension and mental stress melt away, and the solution to a mulled-over problem becomes crystal clear. So if you get out of your La-Z-Boy, you can live ten years longer. The type of exercise doesn't matter as long as you're consistent and stick to it. Whether it's stretching, walking, running, or even gardening, you get to choose health over the La-Z-Boy—and that's a great choice!

DIAL BACK

Most gainfully employed laborers have some type of job stress. If you're a workaholic, though, work stress is a double whammy for you because of the grueling perspective you bring to a task.

Studies show work stress can turn you into a disgruntled worker, making you less effective at what you do. If you toil longer hours at your desk than colleagues, you're at greater risk for anxiety, depression, and burnout and have twice the number of health-related problems compared to those who reduce their work hours.

To cut health risks, you can consider dialing back on overtime and toiling by the adage of working smarter, not longer. You can think of your work site as the Olympics. Your physical and mental endurance at work hinges on being in good shape. You can boost your stamina for workdays by priming with good nutrition, vigorous exercise, and ample sleep.

MAY

STRESS SMARTER

Does it really matter if you don't get the best table at that restaurant? If you miss the first five minutes of the baseball game? Probably not. But when you're used to stress, it becomes second nature—so much so, you might not even realize you're sweating the small stuff!

You might even ask if you're struggling with stress or *eustress*—good stress that motivates you, makes you feel alive, and helps you thrive as you meet challenges. It helped Meryl Streep snag her Oscars, Michael Phelps win his gold medals, and Tom Brady champion his string of Super Bowl wins. So a little eustress gives you thrill and excitement and is a good thing to have. If you notify your nervous system which kind of stress you're up against, you find that usually it's not as bad as you think.

DITCH WHAT-IFS

If you're like most people, chances are you continue to be afraid for reasons long past. And your body still carries the reflex of the old scars—a flip-flop in the stomach, tightness in the chest, a "what-if" in the brain. These intrusive thoughts interrupt your enjoyment of the present and keep you stuck in the future.

Asking "what-if" questions is another form of cat-astrophic thinking that recycles past fears through current time. Most never happen. Asking has become a habit, and you have grown more comfortable with the what-ifs because they keep you on red alert and compel you to try to control unpredictable future out-comes. What-ifs expand when you turn them over and over in your mind. Your thoughts become distorted to the point that you're dealing with a magnification of the problem—not the real problem.

By ditching your what-ifs you save yourself a lot of hand-wringing and wasted time that you could put into work. If you wait to draw conclusions *after* instead of *before* the hard evidence is in, you learn that "what is" usually contradicts "what if."

BE COURAGEOUS

Sometimes you're uncertain of which direction to take when job demands nip at your heels. Being willing opens you up to possibilities and makes you agreeable to change old habits that haven't worked. You're open to changes even though you might not know the com-plete nature of them. You're prepared to relinquish the need to control, to be perfect, and the compulsion to spend your time rushing and doing instead of listen-

MAY

ing and watching. After you surrender your excessive work habits, you show a willingness to let a Higher Power guide you to changes that bring fulfillment and serenity.

Try this exercise: close your eyes and go within. With openheartedness, imagine opening your arms and being willing to accept whatever changes life brings your way—the pleasant along with the unpleasant. Cultivate the belief that you have the courage within you to handle change in whatever form it comes.

ZOOM OUT

Do you look at life through a zoom lens or a wide-angle lens? When your mind zeros in, it magnifies problems and hardships. The wide-angle lens is expansive and helps you see more possibilities.

Identify a complaint you have about your life or yourself. Perhaps you think your mutual fund isn't worth enough, or you worry that you'll have to pull several all-nighters to get caught up at work. Once you identify the complaint, think about the bigger picture. As you broaden your outlook, how important is the judgment you've made against your life? Usually you will find that the complaint loses its sting when you put it in a wider context.

The lens of your mind—not your life conditions—

determines your level of discontent. Once you can see a situation from more than one standpoint, clarity heightens, misery dissipates, and inner peace dwarfs the actual circumstances of your life.

DON'T TELE-PRESSURE YOURSELF

Tele-pressure is the urge to respond immediately to work-related messages no matter when they come. When a device rings, you might not be able to resist the urge to answer because it activates the stress response and gives you a surge of dopamine. Tele-pressure worsens sleep, creates high burnout levels, and results in more health-related absences from work.

Try muting electronics on breaks and after work, so you're not duped by the red alert chime of your devices when they interrupt personal hours. Use custom ringtones for family and friends in order to screen calls, and confine wireless devices to specific areas of your home during off-hours. Ease up on the instant messaging so you don't create the expectation that you're available 24/7.

TAKE A GUILT-FREE TRIP

Only 57 percent of Americans take their earned vacations. You could be one of them who hauls tons of

MAY

work on leisure trips or refuses vacations altogether because extra work responsibilities make it too stressful. You have to get ahead of the workload before you leave and work doubly hard when you get back. So you say the time off isn't worth it. But it is.

The whole point of a vacation is to restore your mind and body and get a new lease on life. Setting boundaries is the ticket. Limited communication with the office while vacationing can be less stressful than worrying about things piling up.

Start by taking your vacation days. Then, when you're out of office, impose work limits on vacation (for example, an hour a day to check emails or make phone calls). Don't work right up until the moment you leave and head back to work right after the plane. If possible, schedule an extra day off before you depart and another when you return to ease back into routines.

MANAGE BAD BOSS VIBES

Studies show that if you have a negative interaction with your boss, the heart takes a hit and blood pressure shoots up. This is often the result of rumination in which you play the negative situation over and over in your head. When a boss berates you, the effect carries over into your personal time after hours.

Your boss might have power over your job, but he or she doesn't have power over your life. You always have the choice of whether you act or react in negative situations. Reacting is a knee-jerk response to threats, whereas acting requires you to take conscious charge of your life. When you act, you remember that the power that dwells within you is greater than the challenges you face in the workplace.

You don't have to wait for the company to decide what's reasonable for you. You can evaluate your job and decide for yourself. How far are you willing to go to meet a boss's unreasonable demands? Are you prepared to act instead of react the next time you have an uncomfortable interchange with your supervisor?

STACK YOUR POSITIVITY DECK

When you have uplifting thoughts on a regular basis, they have cumulative benefits that trump your negative thoughts. Scientists call this the broaden-and-build effect. If you want to blunt job stress, weather workplace challenges, and cultivate work/life balance, here are some cards you can use to stack your positivity deck:

- Step back from negative thoughts and broaden your scope by brainstorming a wide range of possible solutions.

MAY

- Pinpoint the upside in each downside of a negative job challenge.
- Practice encouraging self-talk to counter negative self-judgments.
- Focus on the positive aspects of your life where you can make a difference.
- Hang out with positive coworkers and friends. Like negativity, positivity rubs off on you.
- Fist pump every time you reach a milestone or important work achievement to affirm how awesome you are.
- Never pass up or underestimate the opportunity to persevere in a job crisis. It's all about how you look at it, and your uplifting thoughts can make all the difference.

REMAIN CALM AND CARRY ON

Staying calm when hit with a big challenge is as difficult as resisting the urge to scratch an itch. It takes practice. The truth is, work frustrations and disappointments can hijack your emotions and cause you to react in unhealthy ways. By experiencing disappointment without acting out, you keep from adding insult to injury.

How many times have you been in the middle of an activity that required your full attention when someone interrupted you? Chances are you became irritated. Perhaps you blew up. Equanimity helps you recognize that you are irritated without reacting with anger. With regular practice, you learn you don't have to react every time you are annoyed or disappointed.

PUT DOWN YOUR GAVEL

When you make a mistake or have a setback at work, judging yourself creates another layer of stress, making you more likely to give up. Facing an upsetting situation with impartiality reduces the degree of stress. Self-judgment throws you into a cycle of setbacks: "I ate a piece of carrot cake" spirals into "I've already blown my diet so I might as well eat a second piece," which morphs into "I'm such a loser; I'll never get this weight off." It's not eating the cake but the self-judgment that makes you feel bad. And the bad feelings throw you into a cycle of seeking comfort in the very behavior you're trying to conquer.

The next time your self-judgment pops up after a letdown, try not to steamroll over it. Instead, acknowledge the unpleasant feeling by whispering something impartial like, "Hello, judgment. I see you're active today." This simple acknowledgment will calm down an unpleasant state of mind.

DON'T ISOLATE YOURSELF

Many times you might feel you're the first to go through a particular experience: job loss, breakup, rejection. When you isolate yourself from others, you think your feelings are unique to you and that no one else could possibly understand.

You need a support system so you don't feel isolated. Close friends know how difficult it is to maintain work/life balance, and instead of judging you, they hold empathy. But when you spend too much time working, you fail to develop or maintain that support.

Do you have someone in whom you can confide your mistakes and concerns? If not, examine whether you've isolated yourself to the point that you feel on the outside of life. Then put effort into connecting with someone whom you trust and feel safe with and who gives you encouragement to stay the course.

In your daily readings, online Workaholics Anonymous meetings, or talks with sponsors, you start to realize you're not alone. When you can understand the pain of someone else, it helps minimize your own. When you feel understood by another person, it comforts you and helps you to navigate rough waters.

PUT ON THE BRAKES

Life never moves fast enough for you if you're always rushing. You don't know your limitations and drive yourself beyond human endurance. By approaching work with a slow hand, you can accomplish more, do a better job, and maintain your health. Here are some dos and don'ts to slow down and put on the brakes.

DO: Consider ways to slow down the pulse of your life. Set aside times to eat, walk, and drive slower. Be willing to say no when you're already overloaded. For every new work commitment you take on, eliminate one from your to-do list. Recognize your internal pressure to stay busy doing something and take time to come up for air. Take mindful deep breaths from your diaphragm periodically throughout your workday.

DON'T: Refuse to let someone else's emergency become your crisis. Avoid juggling several tasks at once, since single tasking is more productive than multitasking. If you start to feel restless watching the paint dry, practice just acknowledging and being with the agitation.

MAY

CAPITALIZE YOURSELF

Do you think of yourself as i or I? That might sound like a silly question, but it isn't. If you think of yourself as lowercase, as small and insignificant, it will show through in all aspects of life. If you think you're too small to make a difference, follow the advice of the Dalai Lama, "Try sleeping with a mosquito."

The size of your frame, whether you're male or female, gay or straight, or thin or bulked out—none of that really matters when it comes to your ability. You have to treat yourself first-rate inside your skin instead of crouching in your negotiations, your demeanor, your self-talk, and the ways in which you allow the workplace to treat you.

Holding yourself in high esteem, being your own cheerleader, giving yourself an "atta-boy" or "atta-girl"—all are important for work/life balance. Take a few minutes to contemplate thinking of yourself as upper case, as powerful and deserving. Then notice what happens inside.

SILENCE THE ALARM

Chances are you approach tasks as if you're under threat. When you're not chained to the desk, red alert also flashes inside even when there's no reason for it. It's simple biology: your limbic system is designed to exaggerate your fears and worries for your protection and survival. The limbic system (or lizard brain) throws your prefrontal cortex offline and floods you with stress chemicals.

Once you're aware that your survival brain is on alert, you can take a breath, step back, and get curious. Curiosity helps you gain clarity about why you feel threatened for no good reason. Ask yourself "What am I afraid of?" or "What are the chances of that really happening?" or "What is the worst thing that could happen?"

Abdicating self-judgment and acting with assurance rather than alarm keeps you from attacking yourself and makes it easier to see what's really going on. The brain's executive function kicks back in, creating an impartial bird's-eye view of how you're unwittingly creating stressful situations for yourself.

OUTLAST BURNOUT

If you're burning the candle at both ends, you could be headed for burnout—the physical exhaustion and depletion of emotional energy brought on by the absence of work/life balance. Fortunately, self-care can slow your pace and recharge your batteries—just think of self-care practices as letting up on the gas pedal and putting on the brakes so you don't slam into a wall.

MAY

Putting on the brakes and recharging your batteries prepares you to be more productive, effective, and all-around happier in life.

Set aside time each day to relax, exercise, play, meditate, pray, do yoga, take a trek around the block, or just watch the grass grow. Make a to-be list alongside your to-do list. What will you put on it?

BE RESILIENT

When things go south, as they inevitably will, do you find yourself crumbling under the hard knocks? Do you struggle with fear of making the wrong decision, or are you able to recover and move on?

Work resiliency lets you persevere after ninety-nine rejections so you can succeed on the one hundredth try. From time immemorial, all the great thinkers in every field of endeavor have espoused the same wisdom one way or another: "Never give up." The tide often turns just when you're ready to throw in the towel. Making a mark in the work world is tough and requires cultivating a zone of resilience.

After a failure to achieve a goal, you might tell yourself you can't go on and want to give up. You don't really want to give up. It just feels like that's the only option. But it isn't. You haven't actually even failed; that's just what you call it because your expectations aren't met. You're simply traversing a valley most people go through until they reach the mountain of success.

ADMIT WRONGDOING

Step 5 of Workaholics Anonymous says, "We admitted to God, to ourselves, and to another human being the exact nature of our wrongs." All of us make mistakes. You'll find that the hard part is admitting them and living with the consequences. Maybe your over-doing walled you off from friends or caused you to neglect family members. Or perhaps you developed controlling habits that excluded cooperative co-workers eager to perform as a team. Admitting when you're wrong allows you to forgive yourself with all of your human imperfections. Sharing your short-comings with a loved one, a close business associ-ate, or a group of recovering workaholics liberates you from self-condemnation and from the need to justify, rationalize, minimize, or attack. You become more honest with yourself and acknowledge your past self-righteous behaviors without guilt or self-condemnation.

You won't ever stop making mistakes, but you can stop denying them. No matter how hard you try, you will never be perfect, but you can strive for excellence. When you do make mistakes, it's important to stop beating yourself up and seize the opportunity to learn and do better next time. A fuckup is a glorious teacher, and you can use it in your favor. It gives you an opportunity to acknowledge your humanity—a chance to admit when you're wrong and make giant strides toward integrity. If you didn't make mistakes, how could your know your honest human condition or see the ways your actions harm others? If you avoid the pain of your human failures, you automatically avoid your growth. Without facing the truth, how could you find new ways to be the best person you can be and live a happy and fulfilling life?

MAY TAKEAWAYS

- Put exercise and movement at the top of your list or stand while you work to offset prolonged hours of sitting at a desk.

- Practice promptly admitting your wrongdoings or shortcomings to yourself and others without self-condemnation and watch your integrity grow.

- Set boundaries so you're more effective and fulfilled at work, home, and play.

- Begin each day with an attitude of "yes" instead of "no"—a willingness to live with life's uncertainty and open-mindedness to whatever joys, challenges or disappointments come your way.

- Take vacations instead of guilt trips to restore your mind and body and to get a new lease on life.

- Take time out each day for self-care, mindful contemplation, and self-reflection.

JUNE

To surrender to too many demands, to commit oneself to too many projects, to want to help everyone in everything, is to succumb to violence.

—THOMAS MERTON

ENLIGHTENMENT

In the sunny month of June, the summer solstice marks the longest day of the year, and you are halfway through the twelve months. Think of June as a time of fiery enlightenment when your consciousness burns more brightly in your awareness. Be willing to remove harmful work habits that have kept you mired in addiction—perhaps some of the unhealthy character traits you identified in the month of April, such as impatience, restlessness, perfectionism, and the inability to relax. These traits are not you. They are automatic and impulsive parts of you that make unmindful decisions, are not in your best interest, and eclipse the real you.

Like moths to a flame, workaholics are attracted to high-pressure jobs and lightning speed in the workplace. If this sounds familiar, you probably add to the stress by overloading yourself with more than you can handle. Something Buddhists call Right View can help you become ready to change old thoughts and actions that held you in a state of turmoil. Led by Right View, you learn to be mindful of your unhealthy work habits, pay attention to the types of workaholic

#CHILL

environments that attract you, and thrive. One mindfulness practice that teaches you to chill is called *open awareness*–peacefully observing everything you do to raise your awareness of what's happening moment to moment in the flow of your daily activities such as mindful working, walking, and eating.

Starting now, I invite you to reflect on your workaholic parts that have taken over your life, led you to make unhealthy decisions, and kept you from living a full, integrated life. It's not as hopeless as you might think. Once you're willing to shine a light inward, it's possible to correct these old patterns and cultivate new ones that support work/life integration. You are aided by open awareness as you go through your daily routines, noticing, for example, the sensations of your feet against the ground as you make your way from the parking garage to the office and the feel of the open sky and sights and sounds around you.

As you read this month's meditations, think of shining a curious light on the parts of yourself that have quietly kept you in the dark. Enlightenment makes it possible for you to make healthy changes, connect with your deeper True Self, and see yourself as whole. Once there, you notice more of yourself, refuse to downplay your potential, and value serenity and lightheartedness as much as toil and striving.

START AT DAY ONE

This open awareness exercise can help you slow down and become more mindful of your body, mind, and spirit during your workday:

The next time you go to your work site, imagine it is again the first day. Notice the entranceway, the architecture of the outside and inside of the building, and the people at their workstations as if you've never seen them before, appreciating them with renewed interest. What sounds do you hear and what smells fill the air? Be mindful of the facial expressions of your business associates. Look beyond their eyes into the heart of their souls and register what's imprinted there. Notice if you feel judgment or compassion for the people and situations you're observing. Whatever you feel, try not to judge yourself for the feelings.

STOP BEING A WORKPLACE COMPLAINER

Workplace complainers take adversity personally and believe there's nothing they can do about it. It's important to recognize that the habit of bellyaching can prevent you from making it far up the career ladder. If you lean toward being a pessimistic complainer, try not to take workplace hardships personally. And focus on how you can find solutions to obstacles instead of complaining about them.

JUNE

Even when work is challenging and stressful, your mindset can carry you a long way. Pay attention to the attitude you bring to work or home and try to keep it in check. Take a minute to contemplate one or two negative hardships that work handed you. See if you can pinpoint something you gained from the challenges. Then name other positive aspects of your work that you look forward to and enjoy.

AVOID COMPARING YOURSELF

When you use someone else's life as a yardstick to evaluate your own, you end up judging yourself unfairly and come out on the short end of the stick.

When you compare yourself to the successes of others, you automatically demote yourself. And you believe the comparison even if others hold you in high regard. The way out of this cycle is to rejoice in the prosperity of colleagues at the same time you value your own good fortune and special qualities. Throw modesty out the window and take time now to consider your special traits and unique gifts. Then ask yourself if you believe in them. If not, how can you refine your attitude so that you affirm yourself and perform with more balance, hence more optimally?

CULTIVATE SELF-COMPASSION

I bet you wouldn't dream of treating a loved one the way you treat yourself: pelting yourself for the smallest human mistakes, disbelieving in your abilities, or judging yourself harshly. A compassionate inner voice helps you cope as much as applying salve to a wound.

Start to watch how often you put yourself down. Then start to embrace the punitive voice with a nurturing voice: *Easy does it. You've got this. Just breathe and take your time. You're going to be just fine.* This practice frees up positive emotions such as enthusiasm, interest, inspiration, and excitement, and gives you more confidence to meet daily pressures.

MEET YOURSELF IN THE MIDDLE

Chances are you categorize work and life into extremes of black and white, without realizing it, blinding yourself to the shades of gray where truth usually lies.

When you get stuck in workaholic black-and-white thinking, try letting yourself find the gray area—that dot somewhere in-between the extremes known as the middle way—to give yourself greater work/life balance. "I must do my job perfectly or I won't do it at all" becomes "I don't have to be perfect in everything. I can take risks and learn from my mistakes."

#CHILL

After dedicated practice of looking for the gray, you start to notice the middle way with greater clarity and more compassion toward yourself and bring your work and personal lives into a healthy balance. Why not meet yourself in the middle?

AVOID WORKAHOLIC CULTURE

It's important for you to not only be mindful of your work patterns but also to pay attention to the types of work environments that attract you. Workaholics are attracted to and thrive in high-pressured jobs that put production above employee well-being. When looking for a new job, search for positions that put employee welfare at the highest level of consideration. Look for places that emphasize health and wellness, the ones that also want you to have a life outside of the office. It takes awhile to research companies online before interviews, but remember: looking out for your own happiness is the best kind of homework you can do!

CELEBRATE YOUR ACCOMPLISHMENTS

Many workaholics suffer from *imposter syndrome*—the inability to internalize career accomplishments. You think you're a fraud, able to fool people that you're competent or talented, even though you have yet to convince yourself. Beneath the imposter syndrome lies the belief that you're unworthy and deeply flawed, and you live with a persistent fear of being exposed. Even when situations contradict these notions, you discount them in order to maintain your self-image. In order to feel worthy, you overload yourself with work, hoping you will start to view yourself in the same positive light that others do.

Find reasons to be proud of yourself; think about your accomplishments and all of your hard work. There's plenty to celebrate when you let go of the feelings of inadequacy and embrace achievement instead.

CHILL YOUR CONTROL CRAVING

The need for control is the hallmark of work addiction. You believe you're the only one who can solve a problem when the truth is that it could be delegated. Once a project is out of your hands, you feel a loss of control. It can be hard to trust another person to do a task that you know you can do well.

Instead of overplanning, try to be spontaneous and a little more flexible. When you can't control what's happening, challenge yourself to chill and focus on controlling how you respond to what's happening—instead of everything around you.

BE PATIENT WITH YOURSELF

When it's time to change, it can be easy to try to hurry your decisions to turn a new leaf, though this can lead to disastrous results. You cannot expect to change old thoughts and habits in one day, week, or even a month. It takes a long time to become a workaholic, and recovery from work addiction takes time, too.

When you find yourself becoming impatient with the speed of your own progress, the simple phrase "one step at a time" helps you navigate through a sea of frustration and immobilization. Your progress continues when you can admit to yourself that you're powerless to make things move faster than they already are.

GET RESTORATIVE REST

When overworking is the norm, relaxation is an afterthought. However, rest strengthens your ability to think creatively, to be a team player, and lets you recharge your batteries.

Restorative rest gives you the work/life balance to succeed in all areas of your life. It is passive rest in which your mind is in a state similar to waking sleep with slowed heartbeat and breathing. It allows you to take a break and perform self-care with activities that take you out of your 24/7 work life and clear out your head. Make restorative rest part of your routine, so you can find those moments without imperative in which you don't need anything to be different.

LET YOURSELF LAUGH

Sometimes it might feel irresponsible to take a lighter approach to life. Laughter and fun seem contradictory to getting the job done. Your grim, humorless determination makes you think life has to be all work and no play. You might even look down at people who laugh, tell jokes, or create lightheartedness in the office. But when you forget to laugh at yourself and see the humorous side of life, you allow busyness to siphon the joy from your life.

Living in balance requires you to open yourself to having a good time. A dash of humor doesn't subtract from your productivity; it adds spice to a stressful workday, lightens your workload, and improves productivity and morale. The secret sauce for a delicious, more balanced workday is one or more big belly laughs to relieve you of job pressures.

When was the last time you had one? That's what I thought. Now, as you become enlightened, is the time to lighten up!

#CHILL

SERVE A COMPLIMENT SANDWICH

It can be difficult to be honest and direct when communicating, so you might instead deny that problems exist or communicate your problems in subtle and indirect ways. Maybe you drop casual hints, use nonverbal behaviors, ask someone else to speak for you, or expect others to read your mind.

The compliment sandwich method of communication can help you express difficult feelings or give constructive feedback. Nobody likes to be blasted with negative comments, but if you start with a genuinely positive statement, it makes it easier for the recipient to hear the critique. Then you close with another compliment. This method allows you to give direct feedback in a way that allows others to hear you without defensiveness.

Have you avoided confronting a loved one or employee so much that a divide has widened between you? If so, what communication approaches could you take to mend the relationship? Try this new tool, and allow yourself to bring up your problems and bring healing into your life.

GRAB TIME FOR YOURSELF

You're too busy to spend quality time with your loved ones. You rebuff social invitations because you don't have time. You become irresponsible when it comes to keeping yourself physically and mentally healthy. It's not that you don't have time for yourself, it's that you're not *taking* time for yourself.

The truth is, your first responsibility is to your own health, and recovery from overdoing it shows you how to move your self-care to the top of the list. Try to learn to spend fewer waking hours being an overly responsible worker. Get in the habit of grabbing more time with your family and friends, and living your life more fully.

FIND A NEW PURPOSE

The compulsion to work at the expense of all else is a sickness of the spirit. It can be easy to place all of your life purpose on work, especially when you receive praise for your workplace achievements. Despite this, there's a deep hole inside, a loss of true meaning and purpose.

Constant working becomes a substitute for a true purpose in life by giving you a false sense of security, power, and control over your life. It takes a toll as you experience burnout and a loss of spiritual footing.

Recovery helps you to stop confusing having a career with having a life and to find constructive pastimes. You can find new purpose and meaning through

a deep spiritual connection. Have you lost touch with what's important in life? If so, contemplate some actions you can take to remedy the loss. Find your core values and a purpose that can bring the joy of a chilled and balanced life.

FOCUS ON OUTCOME

Chances are you're less productive when you focus on activity, not outcomes. In many cases, workaholics work for the sake of working and get bogged down with details. Many tasks could be accomplished with less involvement in less time.

You might convince yourself that it's necessary to work on a Saturday to meet a deadline. A chilled worker might exert extra effort during the week, ask for help, or find more efficient ways to approach the task in order to have the weekend free. To the outside world, the workaholic appears to be more involved in the job, but the motive isn't to do better, only to keep doing and dampen unpleasant feelings.

What about you? Does the amount you put into work tasks equal your level of productivity? Could you approach work projects in more efficient ways so you maintain a balance between working and leisure time?

EMBRACE REJECTION

It's hard to deal with rejection when it comes to things you care about. That's why you feel pain about that position you weren't hired for, that exam you didn't pass, or that text you didn't receive after the date you were so excited about. Workplace rejection can especially hurt, such as if management chose a colleague for the promotion over you.

Chances are your work and personal lives involve a lot of rejection at every stage, and it can be devastating. However, success is founded on rejection. In recovery, you learn to accept the opposites of your desires. You learn to accept defeat in the same way you accept winning. After all, you can't have success without defeat. Think of rejection as a stumble, not the end of the road.

Your power resides in how you respond to rejection—not the rejection itself. Remember, you're not alone. Rejection is usually not a personal slap in the face. In fact, it is often an omen of good things to come.

CULTIVATE STRESS HARDINESS

You don't always keep your mind and body in top shape. Maybe you grab fast foods and forget to rest and exercise. Perhaps you are notorious for eating on

JUNE

the run, losing sleep, and ignoring aches and pains that could indicate stress or signal major illness. It's time to start properly fueling your body, so you can deal more healthily with stress.

Scientists link physical fitness to stress hardiness. The holy grail of stress reduction is regular exercise, ample sleep, and good nutrition, which together make you more stress-resistant. When you take the time to make these your lifestyle habits, you'll find you are more tolerant of hassles and minor annoyances such as waiting in lines, traffic snarls, or flight delays. After all, responding to your needs with love and attention provides you the spiritual sustenance to heal mind and body.

WELCOME THE GLORY OF SOLITUDE

Raise your hand if you're supercharged and still on fast-forward after work hours. I thought so. You're not alone. Too many of us don't know how to cut off from work long enough to unwind with solitude. Perhaps you resist being alone and fill your life with hyper-busyness to keep lonely feelings at bay for fear of what you might find lurking inside. You need to properly value the only companion you have from birth to death: yourself.

Loneliness is the poverty of self; solitude is the richness of self. You can start to find peace and serenity through solitude—a sanctuary that you create at home, in your office, or in some other special place where you can meditate and reflect on your life. Solitude replenishes the soil you feel slipping from under your feet from the wear and tear of daily commitments. It helps you become a seawall of strength against the push and pull of daily tides.

CHANGE YOUR PERSPECTIVE

Whether you're a harried parent, driven businessperson, or worried retiree coping with an uncertain future, stressors eventually catch up. It can be easy to hold a negative perspective and focus on what is going wrong.

Instead of focusing on the negative, it's time to challenge yourself to think differently. "I'm paying more taxes this year than ever" becomes "I made more money this year than ever." "I won't go to the party because I won't know anyone" becomes "If I go to the party, I might make new friends." Or when you find good news wrapped around bad news: "My friend's car was totaled" becomes "The car was totaled, but no one was injured."

By taking a different perspective under pressure, you can reshape your way of thinking and train yourself to find the positive side of a situation. In doing so, you can cultivate positive emotions and begin to bring calm into your life.

SEND COMBATIVENESS PACKING

Some days it feels as if work/life balance is a perpetual struggle, one battle after another. When you feel you're constantly fighting and losing, it's time to look at what's going on inside. Sometimes you might unconsciously draw battle lines with your combative attitudes. Maybe you try to force your will on others, resist listening to other points of view, or cling to old ways of doing things. If you're argumentative or overbearing, you create a war within yourself without realizing it.

When something distasteful happens, it's not the situation but the attitude you take that upsets you. The experience isn't good or bad. It just is. The minute you judge it based on your subjective perspective, you become emotionally involved. If you magnify a situation, it could mean you've lost perspective. You learn that many trials are really only trifles.

What combative attitudes need changing? Are you insisting that things be done your way? Do you expect life to deliver on your terms? Are you forcing, resisting, or clinging to the idea that it will make your days acceptable?

CURB YOUR PROCRASTINATION

When you're overwhelmed with work, procrastination becomes one of the go-to methods of handling the load. You could avoid the work out of fear your efforts won't be perfect enough, but then the load grows larger. As the work piles on, you can become anxious, irritable, and even feel self-hatred. In the short term, stalling gives you temporary relief, but in the long run it adds a second layer of pressure, making matters worse.

You're more powerful than your procrastination. You can give yourself permission to be imperfect and make mistakes in order to break the cycle of putting things off. The key is to approach a growing to-do list head-on and early instead of waiting until the last minute. Breaking tasks down and approaching them one by one, instead of focusing on the whole picture, keeps the pile from overpowering you. With several items on your list, decide which are essential and start with the ones you can accomplish quickly to get going.

JUNE

#CHILL

STRIVE TO BE THE REAL DEAL

In Step 6 of Workaholics Anonymous, you become ready to have your imperfections removed. In the attempts to be perfect, you are unable to tolerate mistakes and try to avoid them or cover them up. This dishonesty diminishes your authenticity and ironically creates the imperfection you try to avoid. If you want to be the real deal, your integrity becomes more important to you than your fear of how others perceive you. You admit the exact nature of your shortcomings and learn from them. You are prepared to have them removed and become a master of self-correction.

To be the real deal, you don't have to be the strongest or know the most. You're honest about what you don't know instead of boasting about what you do know. Admitting the exact nature of your wrongs and being open to remove them doesn't mean you put yourself down, or become complacent or irresponsible. Admitting when you're wrong allows you to let go of dishonesty and make peace with your human imperfections. It doesn't diminish your value; it raises your worth and makes you stronger, a more valuable leader. The real deal.

JUNE TAKEAWAYS

- Practice open awareness as you go through your daily routine in order to cultivate a clear and calm mind.

- Outsmart pessimism by looking on the positive side of a negative situation and focusing on the solution instead of the problem.

- Challenge yourself to let go and surrender when you can't control what's happening and focus on the way you respond to what's happening.

- Welcome solitude as an opportunity to bathe yourself in self-reflection or meditation so you can recharge your batteries, change your perspective, and stay cool under pressure.

- Be mindful of the lighthearted side of life to help you chill and achieve more balance.

- Strive to be the real deal—honest and genuine with others and able to admit, correct, and learn from your shortcomings.

JULY

Humbly befriend your busy mind so you don't work your brains out and your brain doesn't work you out.

HUMILITY

The month of July was named after Julius Caesar. For the average person, warm summer days are a time to chill outside—to swim, hike, or barbecue. But workaholics, who feel guilty and anxious when not working, minimize the value of play and ignore outdoor fun or holidays such as July Fourth. What about you? Do you shun socializing, hobbies, and leisure activities? Do you continue to toil inside during the summer months even after colleagues call it quits? If so, July is the time for you to reflect and meditate on how your inability to chill has isolated you and left your ego in charge.

EGO stands for "Ease Good Out." When the ego controls your life, it keeps you from knowing your deeper True Self and prevents you from fully integrating your life. Your ego whispers to you that work is the most important thing in your life and that you're "all that" because you're on top of your game with awards, fat paychecks, and recognition.

In this chapter, I walk you through how to prepare inwardly to make amends to people you have harmed because of your ego's hyperfocus on toiling. Now that you have been enlightened in the month of June, the best medicine for change and transformation is a big

#CHILL

dose of humility. It's difficult to change personal flaws without it. Humility gives you an unfiltered look into yourself so you can see that there's more to you than projects and deadlines. And it gives you an honest perspective that loved ones, friends, and coworkers are more important, too. It helps you renounce the ability to control every person and situation and move from the center of your universe to become a harmonious part of your family, social group, or workplace.

You develop understanding and empathy for those around you, perhaps the ones you've looked down on or ignored. Or the ones you worked hard for so they'd applaud you, see your brilliance, tell you how wonderful you are, or be envious of your success. Starting now, you can chill on a level plane with everyone else and integrate into their lives instead of expecting them to drop everything and blend with yours. You look deeper, willing to feel the pain you medicated for so long with compulsive busyness and overworking. Feeling pain and joy equally make it possible for you to achieve a deeper state of spiritual well-being. And your new way of chilling becomes a giant compliment to your legacy of doing.

During the month of July, you don't stand in the way of anything, you don't overcrowd, and you don't obstruct anything. You think of yourself less and others more. And you are humbled by your journey of modesty instead of trying to be "all that." You leave this chapter with the perspective that work/life balance isn't just about accomplishment and recognition or the absence of upset or disappointment but also your willingness to open your arms and embrace it all.

QUIET YOUR MIND

Being mindful for just two minutes helps you get more acquainted with your urge to get busy. This is the perfect month to get outside, let nature transport you from your artificial world of social media and tasks, and quiet your mind. Even though two minutes might feel like an eternity, it's important to push back against the restlessness.

Try meditating for two minutes on some aspect of nature and feel humbled by it. Watch the grass grow, observe a plant, or fixate on a waterfall. Feel the breeze on your face, notice the colors of flowers, or pay attention to sounds of birds. As the urge to do something bubbles up, don't fight it. Focus on it much like you would isolate a muscle in a workout. Notice how you feel without judging or trying to change the feeling. Ask yourself if the urge is distracting you from or masking other aspects of yourself: anxiety, fear of failure, or intimacy issues. Then bring compassion and humility to whatever it is and see if that quiets your mind.

BEWARE OF WORK BULIMIA

Some people who have out-of-control work patterns that alternate between binges and purges fall into the category of *bulimic workaholics*. Could this be you? If so, faced with a time crunch, you engage in frantic productivity, followed by inertia. You overcommit, wait until the last possible minute, then throw yourself into a panic working frantically to complete a task.

Procrastination and perfectionism are two sides of the same coin of work bulimia. You procrastinate out of fear of not completing a perfect work project. Paralyzed by perfectionism, you go through long periods of work inertia. Yet, while stagnating over getting started, you obsess over the job's completion. Outwardly, it appears you're avoiding work, but inwardly you're working obsessively hard.

When you get overwhelmed, putting things off can eat away at you, making you anxious, irritable—even cause you to dislike yourself. The key is getting started. Choosing just one item from your to-do list that you can complete in a short time lifts the burden of procrastination and motivates you to move on to the next item.

OBSERVE NATIONAL WORKAHOLICS DAY

Every year July 5th marks National Workaholics Day, dedicated to people who spend all their time working and ignore other life pursuits. This day raises awareness that working overtime, skipping lunch, and depriving yourself of sleep is a lethal cocktail for workers nationwide.

On this day you are encouraged to make a lifestyle change and give other aspects of life their due emphasis: play, social activities, hobbies, exercise, sleep, eating healthy foods, and attending to relationships. Otherwise, you're at risk for fatigue, and a fatigued brain has slowed reaction time, poor decision-making ability, and loss of situational awareness and control.

Today is the day to spread the word and educate people about the dangers of work addiction. If you have a workaholic in your life, ask him or her to take a day off and do something fun together: have a meal at a restaurant or go on a hike. If you're a workaholic, take the day off, learn to relax, and contemplate where your work/life balance needs attention. Take a long-needed vacation if you haven't had one in years.

#CHILL

DEVELOP CLARITY

Overworking prevents you from seeing that your addiction has overtaken you and clouded your perceptions. Much like a rail-thin anorexic who looks in the mirror and sees herself as fat, perhaps you scoff at coworkers and family members who accuse you of working too much.

You get so caught up in your subjective experience that you deny the objective perceptions by those around you. The denial allows you to stay stuck in the addiction while eclipsing your clarity of the situation. A chilled worker in an office dreams about being on the ski slopes; a workaholic on the ski slopes dreams about being back in the office.

As you lift the veil of perceptual distortion, the fog of confusion and indecision lifts. You take the perspective of "the beginner's mind" and start to see more clearly inside and out. Take a few minutes now and meditate on assuming "the beginner's mind." See if you can remove your blinders and experience life with more clarity and greater possibilities.

DROP THE DRAMA QUEEN ACT

If you're a workplace drama queen, chances are you put yourself and others under unrealistic deadlines, overload yourself, and try to balance many tasks at once. You spin bite-sized problems into overblown disasters, cry wolf at the slightest obstacle, nitpick over the miserable cards life dealt you, thrive on chaos, and feel like a victim instead of a survivor. While you get an adrenaline and cortisol high from dramatic outbursts, coworkers and subordinates are thrown off-kilter from the stress.

In recovery, drama queens learn that sensationalism isn't a substitute for hard work. You're humbly mindful of any inclination to go into crisis mode, and in a true crisis you remember that misery is *optional,* not *optimal.* You regulate your moods, slow down your work pace, avoid overloading, and refrain from making mountains out of molehills.

WATCH YOUR SELF-TALK

Have you ever had a sinking feeling before a big work moment? That feeling comes from an inner voice predicting you'll mess up or that your concept or presentation won't be received well.

The self-talk is not all of you. It's an aspect of you, but you're much more than the voice, just as there's more to you than your wrist or rib cage. When you notice that you're stuck in an unpleasant emotional state—such as worry, anger, or frustration—try holding that part of you at arm's length and observe it with

#CHILL

an impartial eye. Consider it much as you might notice a blemish on your hand, then ask yourself where it came from. Instead of pushing away the unpleasant feeling, the key is to acknowledge it with something like, "Hello, doubt, I see you're active today."

Why not give it a try now? See if you have a persistent thought or feeling that continues to nag you. Watch it with curiosity as you would a leaf carried downstream over rocks in a brook. Let it come and go without personalizing, resisting, or identifying with it. This approach separates you from the unpleasantness, and it eventually floats away.

FACE YOUR EGO

As you strive to prove your self-worth, everything and everyone becomes a standard against which you measure your ego. Your way of doing something is *the* way. You amplify the triumphs of others into defeat for yourself. You cling to your degrees, titles, or uniforms—but you need to ask yourself what is really important in your life.

It isn't easy to open up and let others see the real you because you're hardwired for ego protection and survival. It takes confidence and courage to risk letting people glimpse your True Self. When you're able to go out on the limb, you find the fruit of the tree. The risk of letting your human spirit shine through removes the ego shield and cultivates more confidence and courage. You'll find that when you live your truth, you have more success and happiness than you ever could have before.

GET ENTHUSIASTIC

If you dread certain aspects of your job, chances are you focus on them before a workday. Whatever you focus on expands. When you focus on dread, it grows bigger inside. But even if you face a day of challenges, you can go to work with the same enthusiasm you have on days without challenges.

When you approach work with enthusiasm, it ignites that spark to get things done. Suppose you ask yourself what aspects of the workday excite you or ignite enthusiasm. Then you focus on those things that bring you joy, passion, or sheer enjoyment.

Is it a favorite coworker or client? Is it a particular place or an interactive situation? See if you can find one positive part of your daily schedule that you look forward to. Then focus on it and let it expand into enthusiasm inside. You will discover more chill time, job success, and personal joy.

#CHILL

ISOLATE YOUR FRAGMENTS

Work addiction is just a fragment of who you are. When you isolate that one fragment, you learn that it's hitched to everything else within you. You don't have to live as a fragment anymore—half-baked and undeveloped. There's so much more to explore. Once you're ready to live more fully and embrace all of yourself, you start to think of work addiction as a fragment separate from you. Then you have the clarity to ask, "Who is the rest of me?" If you don't have an answer, that's okay, too. The good news is that you have plenty of time to explore and find out. That exploration is called recovery.

When you consider work addiction as a fragment of your makeup, you can weave together a beautiful pattern that incorporates all the rest of you. And the brilliant completeness has a clearer meaning when you view it in this new light.

WELCOME CHILL

It's likely that you're more accustomed to chaos than chill. You cringe at the thought of powering down, perhaps even panic when there's nothing to do. You're used to your brain working you fast and furious. Living in a daily grind of work and life pressures doesn't support your slowing down, either.

But if you want to live in optimal balance, you must be in charge of your mind and work, not the other way around. I call this *mindful working*. A calm state helps you cultivate a peaceful center from which to live your life. When you're chilling, your heart rate and respiratory rate slow down. Your mind is open and clear, and actions and decisions are reflective, even, and balanced. As worry and fear recede, a blissful serenity makes everything seem right with the world. It's important to note that you only have bursts of this state. It would be a mistake to think that you can live in a constant state of chill. But the more you practice mindfulness, the more you can access the chill state even in times of upheaval. And the more productive and healthier you become.

BOW DOWN

Most of us experience the pain of self-doubt, rejection, and disappointment from time to time on the job. Humility helps you accept whatever you're reacting to *exactly* as it is. And accepting the outcomes, instead of resisting them, reduces your suffering, empowers you, and frees you.

Think of a disappointment or disillusionment in your work life. Then settle in a quiet place to meditate on the letdown. As you focus on it, spend a few minutes

JULY

imagining yourself as a grain of sand in the universe amid the awesomeness around you. Meditate on the notion that there's something much larger than both you and the letdown. Then bring self-compassion to the disappointment and see if you can accept it in your heart and soul.

REBOOT

A friend told me, "I'm in a job where I'm always behind. You might say if I blinked, I'd be behind, but the truth is, I don't have to blink because I'm always behind." Do you feel snowed under at work? Constantly behind the eight ball?

It's helpful to watch the words you use to express work woes. They give a window into your mind's eye. When you say, "I'm always behind," you can overwhelm yourself with the message that you're somehow at fault, have done something wrong, or aren't doing enough. You have the power to create your *experience* of the job. If you identify as a helpless victim at the mercy of the workplace, you become miserable. If you think of yourself as strong, you can ask, "How am I treating my job?" and notice the shift in how you feel.

My friend removed the oppressive feelings of her job by reframing her work situation with "The position I'm in is one in which many people might feel behind much of the time." Do you need to reboot your mindset so you're not personalizing job stress? When you take away the self-talk's oppressive nature, you free yourself from feeling trapped and enhance your feelings of self-confidence.

GET SHOVEL-READY

Could you be hiding behind your toiling for fear of facing something deep within yourself? That something motivates you to keep plugging away, one task after another, to distract you from digging further into it. If you're a workaholic, you know exactly what I mean. You feel it, don't you—that edginess, restlessness? But you keep pushing it underground, without fully realizing it, and never get down to the essence of it.

At some point, it's essential to start asking questions without judgment: What am I hiding from? Could I be afraid of intimacy because I've been hurt? Is it a fear that people won't like the real me? Am I concerned down deep that I won't be able to measure up? Do I have a deep part of me that says I haven't earned the right to exist? Does my work addiction shield me from overwhelming anxiety?

After some digging, I finally faced what my work addiction distracted me from. And it freed me. Do you know what's underneath? If not, consider digging a little

\#CHILL

further. You won't discover anything that will hurt you. What you find will set you free.

ENJOY GREENER PASTURES

It's a fact. One way for you to chill in your workspace is to enjoy the natural outdoors as much as you can. If you're a workaholic, you're notorious for spending inordinate amounts of time working indoors.

Scientists say outdoor time is the ticket to revitalizing your health. Just twenty minutes a day in a park or natural setting raises and sustains your energy level and recalibrates a fatigued brain. If that's not possible, a view of Mother Nature from a window—scenes of wooded areas, water, sunsets, wildlife, or parks—can lower your heart rate and respiration and relax your muscles.

Consider taking five-minute strolls outside during the workday or up and down a flight of stairs in bad weather. Studies show that you perform better at work after a walk in the woods rather than along a busy street. So find a park or have lunch in a natural setting. Sit by a fountain or go to a zoo when you have a break. Feel the breeze on your face, notice the colors and smells of leaves and flowers, pay attention to chirping crickets, warbling birds, or rushing water.

ACCEPT JOB UNCERTAINTY

Job uncertainty is a certainty for you and everyone you work with. You never know when your company will be sold, your position eliminated, or you will be replaced by someone else. If you're like many people, this uncertainty causes you to refuse to take a lunch hour, earned vacation, or sick days for fear of being perceived as a slacker—a hazard that further contributes to physical and emotional illnesses.

Your best defense against job uncertainty is to manage work stress: make yourself indispensable on the job, keep yourself fit outside of work, find small escapes such as working out or gardening. Take breaks, lunch hours, and vacations. The secret sauce to job uncertainty is to accept that you're not in control of the uncertainty.

Sound counterintuitive? Yes, but when you think about it, many aspects of a job are beyond your control: threat of budget cuts, impending layoffs, or worry over unemployment. Studies show that your inability to accept job uncertainty takes a greater toll on your health than actually losing the job. And your ability to accept job uncertainty reduces work stress, brings peace of mind, and allows you to make the best of your situation.

JULY

BE A GIANT OAK

An acorn contains within it a mighty oak. In the same way, you contain tremendous roots of strength. You can ask yourself if you're in touch with those roots, if you feel like an acorn or a giant oak. It's important to recognize and nurture your strength for it to sprout into the stamina to withstand compulsive working and successful recovery from it.

This doesn't mean physical strength only. I'm talking about the determination and willpower necessary to show up on the job, practice healthy work habits, and balance them with family, friends, and self-care.

When your struggles with overdoing it try to uproot you, remember that you have everything you need to keep your feet planted on the ground and that your deep roots cannot be reached by a hard frost. As you harness all the strength within you, like the gentle bush that digs its roots deep, you can spread upward and split through the compulsive working that holds you down.

WAIT

You might be so accustomed to speeding from task to task that waiting conflicts with your engine speed. You expect people and situations to adapt to your hurried pace. How often do you catch yourself drumming your fingers, clicking your nails, or white-knuckling it through a waiting period?

I developed a quick and easy acronym, WAIT, as a tool to *act* instead of *react* when navigating long lines, waiting rooms, or airline delays.

Watch what's going on inside when you're triggered by waiting stress.

Accept the stressor and inner reactions by saying you're choosing to wait.

Invite the inner reactions to relax and soothe them with curiosity and compassion.

Tell your inner reactions in a mental whisper, "We've got this."

Perhaps you're notorious for reacting with frustration to waiting because it prevents you from completing your to-do list. Once you learn to take a breath and WAIT, it inhibits your automatic reaction, prevents your limbic system from hijacking you, and gives you mindful awareness to chill.

ESTABLISH A WORK-FREE ZONE

No matter how frantic your schedule, you can always take time out to decompress. When you take reflective moments out of each day to spend with yourself, job stress doesn't seem as overwhelming nor life unmanageable. Having a special place to relax free of work stress and negativity makes you more likely to hit the pause button.

Assign a getaway in your home where you're not allowed to think about work issues. Make this work-free zone a place of solitude where you have quiet and serenity. Your zone contains no electronic devices, no work tools, no hassles, and no scheduling boards. Thought streams of worry, rumination, and pressure are off-limits in this special place.

Consider having a room for meditation, prayer, or contemplation. If you don't have a room, find an area with minimum traffic flow. Make an altar containing special mementos and favorite photographs that raise pleasant memories and peaceful feelings. A corner of a den or bedroom where you wear earphones and listen to relaxing music works as a getaway. If you want to go whole hog, make your bathroom a spa for a few hours. Place scented candles around the tub, play soft music, and draw a warm bath with essential oils or rose petals.

KEEP AN UNKEPT STATISTIC

If you're married to a workaholic, has your spouse ever thrown you under the bus so he or she could overwork? If so, those actions follow a common pattern among spouses of workaholics. You may have felt alone, but you're not.

Spouses of workaholics report more marital estrangement, emotional withdrawal, and thoughts of separation and divorce. They are 45 percent more likely to divorce. They feel neglected, shut out, unloved, and unappreciated due to a workaholic spouse's physical and emotional remoteness.

Have you put your life on hold because of a workaholic mate? If so, you could be enabling the very addiction you wish to erase from your life. Many spouses build their lives around the workaholic because they want to feel connected and supportive. That's natural, right? Not with workaholics.

Postponing your life only leads to disappointment and enabling. When your workaholic promises to be home in time for dinner and never shows (for the umpteenth time), consider eating on time without him. Refrain from such activities as bringing your loved one work when she goes to bed sick, making alibis for her absenteeism or lateness at social functions or family gatherings, or assuming his household duties.

JULY

#CHILL

WELCOME THE REMOVAL

Step 7 of Workaholics Anonymous says, "We humbly asked God to remove our shortcomings." The key word here is humility. Without humility, you don't have the vision essential for growth, and progress in your recovery is unlikely. But if you're ready to have your acknowledged shortcomings removed, humility can help you remove them.

It's possible that at one time or another you beat your chest and believed you're so special that you are exempt from the rules that others must follow. In recovery, you're honest about how your ego has taken over your work and personal lives. You realize that the faults of others are like car headlights that only seem more glaring than your own. You no longer point a finger at the mistakes of others but shine a light on yours. You put yourself on an equal plane with fellow human beings by admitting you have the same flaws.

You humbly work on your imperfections. True spiritual progress is yours as you humbly submit to the same standards as everyone else. As old shortcomings melt away, work associates, family, and friends respond to you in new and more approving ways.

JULY TAKEAWAYS

- Emancipate yourself from your ego so you can make free choices to chill your spirit.

- Be vigilant for your ego's penchant to be a drama queen and avoid crisis mode.

- Practice humility in all of your affairs.

- Learn to WAIT, slow down, and chill with life's curveballs.

- Refuse to hide behind work to shield you from facing something inside yourself.

- Create a work-free zone where you can quiet your mind and chill.

- Remember that EGO stands for "Ease Good Out" and integrate your work life with your True Self.

AUGUST

Sometimes your biggest obstacles lie between your own two eyes. Step out of your comfort zone, out of your own way, and admit when you're wrong.

ADMITTING HARM

Named after the Roman emperor Augustus, the month of August is a time of completion—a time for you to tie up loose ends, heal past relationships, and envision a clearer future. The word *august* describes something or someone who is honorable, noble, or esteemed. To live up to these attributes, you break the mold of your comfort zone and take new actions to situations you have closed yourself off to until now.

Your compulsion *to do* has overpowered your desire *to be*, turning you into a human doer instead of a human being. Your mind has lived in the past and future, missing the present moment altogether. It's difficult for you to relax and unwind, do nothing, and enjoy the now. You end up hurting people around you as well as yourself.

In keeping with the theme of being honorable and noble, the eighth month encourages you to make a list of everyone you have harmed (including yourself) and become willing to make amends to them all: the time you jumped down the office assistant's throat for forgetting to FedEx an important letter; the evening you worked late and missed your son's piano recital; the day you scolded your spouse who wanted to spend time with you for interrupting your train of thought; the episodes when you abused yourself working around the clock, shaking your fist at the heavens, pissed that there weren't more hours in the day.

This chapter takes you on a life review of sorts as you look up from your desk, put down your iPhone, and take time out for mindful contemplation. Who did you hurt and why? And how did you hurt them? As you contemplate what Buddhists call Right Intention, you become willing to give up the true causes of your suffering—the craving of power and productivity and material trappings that separate you from yourself and others. Your willingness to make amends to all people you harmed shifts something inside. Your honest vulnerability activates more lovingkindness that lets you forgive those you have hurt and forgive yourself for having hurt them. And you're able to chill.

As you consider this exercise, it's helpful to notice what you discover about yourself. Are you resistant to the idea? Have you already started to judge yourself? Does the thought of the exercise create overwhelming feelings? If possible, try to accept whatever reaction you have with self-compassion, nonjudgment, and forgiveness.

After mindful contemplation, you make a list of

the family members, friends, and coworkers (including yourself) you have hurt. What damage has frantic living done to your physical and mental health or the mental health of others? Perhaps emotional repercussions lie in the wake of your excessive working. Do you have friends or loved ones who feel rejected or abandoned because you weren't there for them? If so, now is the time to put them on your repair list and get ready to make amends to them. It's also the time to contemplate forgiving yourself for the burdens of harm you've carried for so long. As a result of your vulnerable actions this August, you start to feel more honorable, noble, and esteemed.

LEARN TO UNWIND

It's difficult to do nothing when idle time makes you feel anxious and unproductive. You are apt to avoid the unpleasantness by getting busy again. But change comes when you do something different in the heat of the moment.

Here's a mindful relaxation exercise that you can practice for ten to twenty minutes to help you unwind: Sit quietly in a comfortable position with eyes closed. Starting at your feet and progressing up to your face, deeply relax all of your muscles. Pay close attention

AUGUST

#CHILL

to your breathing. Breathe in easily and naturally through your nose. As you breathe out through your mouth, say the word *chill* silently to yourself. As distracting thoughts occur, try to ignore them and return to repeating "chill" with each exhalation.

After you've finished, sit quietly for several minutes at first with your eyes closed, then with your eyes slowly opening. Avoid judging yourself based on how successful you were. If possible, practice mindful relaxation once or twice daily.

STOP STRETCHING TIME

How often do you hear the refrain, "There're just not enough hours in a day"? Your need to stretch time as if it's a rubber band is a reflection of your need to overdo, your inability to accept life on its own terms. You try to push the river instead of letting it flow by itself. You try to force more hours than there are into the workday.

Your life becomes more manageable when you structure your workdays for only twenty-four hours and learn to work, sleep, and play within those boundaries. Studies show that workaholics with work/life balance accomplish in fifty hours what they previously couldn't do in eighty. When you live within natural timelines, you're less stressed, just as productive, and have more time for work/life balance and spiritual reflection.

DON'T THROW STICKS AND STONES

As a child, we used to chant, "Sticks and stones can break my bones, but names will never hurt me." Of course, it wasn't true. Words cut deeply, and you can do great damage to others—and to yourself—with hateful comments. On the flip side, kind words and loving affirmations and affectionate support can do more to soothe and mend an injured spirit than human medicine.

Do you use your tongue to condemn or to uplift, heal, and support? Start to pay attention to how you talk to yourself. Are your words building you up or tearing you down? As you notice how you treat yourself and others, ask with compassion what you need to do to change what you say.

CHECK THE FLIP SIDE

The practice of flipping a negative situation enables you to see the granule of good: more beauty than flaws, more hope than despair, more blessings than disappointment. Once you realize things happen as they're supposed to happen, you can start to accept them at face value and know that some good is being born.

AUGUST

At times you forget, make a mistake, or say something wrong because you're human. If you treat yourself with compassion, instead of condemnation, you turn your mistakes into lessons from which to learn. Asking how you can adjust from your shortcomings flips your perspective and builds you up instead of tearing you down.

KNOW YOUR OTHER KNOWING

A logical mind is a wonderful tool. The ability to think, analyze, and predict is the cornerstone of career success. But the rational mind carries you only so far in your recovery. Too much logic is like too much salt in the soup. It makes things difficult to swallow.

If you work excessively, you spend a disproportionate amount of time in your head making decisions. But some life dilemmas require you to look into your heart. When you're dealing with feelings and intimacy, resorting to the rational mind doesn't work.

A dash of intuition brings the zest of balance to your life. You discover that you must balance your logical mind with intuition—the other knowing. You've heard people say, "I know in my heart I did the right thing." This other knowing is your inner wisdom, separate from the mind. It requires that you turn to your heart for important emotional decisions. You can't dissect the other knowing. You can't examine it under a microscope, but it's alive and well inside all of us.

USE YOUR HANDS

Your hands are the servants of the mind. They are the sculptors of your life. Take a few minutes to look at your hands and consider how powerful they are. Imagine holding a sculpting knife in front of a huge lump of clay. You have the freedom to carve your life in many different ways.

Your hands have the power to sculpt a life of bliss or a pit of misery. How many times have you relinquished your sculpting knife to people or situations that whittle you away? Do your hands a favor. Look at them and the lump of clay before you again. Think about the power you have to sculpt your life. As you hold the carving knife, what does your mind need to do so your hands can create the life you really want? Work less? Work smarter? Play more? Take better care of yourself? Repair brittle relationships? Take time off? What then?

CREATE A VACUUM

Some of life's most stunning moments are unplanned. They happen spontaneously when you allow an empty space in your life for them to come in. Nature abhors

AUGUST

CHILL

a vacuum. When your life is packed to the hilt, too frantic, and fast moving, your control blocks out the magical moments. All you have to do to let life's magic in is to open up.

Think about creating a vacuum in your life. What can you move out of your life that takes up space to make room for your growth? Could it be an old relationship, dinosaur attitudes, stuffed emotions, bad work habits, a cluttered desk?

What are you ignoring or holding on to that you can empty so you're in a position to receive life's miracles? Do you have a welcome space to chill—a place for new and healthier attitudes, emotions, and actions?

STOP STEAMROLLING

Are you so determined to complete tasks and reach deadlines that you ride roughshod over other people's opinions? Do you stampede over anyone who dares to offer a different way of conducting business, paying the bills, or cutting grass? Do you leave coworkers, family members, or friends in the dust without stopping to consider their perspectives?

The problem with this approach is that your way isn't necessarily the best way. Perhaps you just think it is. You want the job done "right," so you take the reins and refuse to delegate. Then you move on to the next item on your to-do list. Steamrolling ideas to get to resolution prevents you from being a team player, listening to other viewpoints, or realizing that your ideas can be just as stale or off the mark as the next person's.

Work/life integration entails taking time to engage in the process of working with others as a team member. You avoid diving into projects or rushing job decisions. You take time to think through facts before finalizing plans. In recovery from overdoing it, you learn to engage in creative brainstorming, not premature self-centered steamrolling.

ENTER THE UNKNOWN ZONE

In addition to lunch, there's one other thing all of us carry to our work desks: the unknown. Like most people, you probably count on predictability. Perhaps your very survival depends on it. You want to know when, where, and how things will happen. But you can't always know if you will get the raise, the promotion, or good review.

Your attitude toward the unknown can either propel you to success or sabotage your career. Welcoming it with open arms is your best course of action because it's one of the few things you can count on. Things won't always go as planned. Unexpected events will

AUGUST

#CHILL

blindside you, and you will experience disappointments and rejections. If that's unacceptable, you end up arguing with life instead of living it.

When you avoid grasping for certainty to cushion a fall, you won't succumb to fear of the unknown. And you gain a peace of mind that contributes to the quality of your work. This acceptance sustains you through work/life challenges and frees you from the clutches of your own spewing torrent of self-doubt.

Contemplate the unknown in your life. Consider the risk of welcoming it with openheartedness. Try to accept future unknowns, using them to grow fully into the chilled person you aspire to be.

SALUTE IMPERFECTION

Contrary to what you tell yourself, most people don't expect you to be perfect. Your flawed perceptions lead you to go overboard—far beyond what colleagues and business organizations expect. Sometimes what you consider an adequate effort far outweighs the expectations of others.

It's time to stop the self-abuse. Ask yourself what you can do to view your capabilities in more realistic ways and set reachable goals. Your best work isn't perfection; it's your best work. That's good enough and as good as it gets.

SWALLOW YOUR PRIDE

When your ego tries to protect you from failure, humiliation, or wrongdoing, it can reek of conceit and arrogance. Perhaps you hide the news of a job rejection at Amazon but broadcast to everyone the position you nabbed at Yahoo. It's difficult to admit you're wrong or didn't get what you wanted, even though you worked so hard for it.

A bitter pill indeed to swallow your pride. Gulp! But letting it go makes you more successful at work and in your personal life. When you can open your heart and accept the vulnerability of being authentic, you release a burden. Ultimately, it's better to lose your pride with a close coworker or loved one than to lose them because of your senseless pride.

You will make mistakes, say things you regret, and hurt others. It's inevitable. But you don't have to let pride cover up your wrongdoing. Choosing the path of humility and courage, instead of ego and pride, makes you a stronger leader in the workplace and a more loving family member at home.

GO GRAY

One of the biggest fears workaholics have with work/life balance is that they must slash work hours, change careers, or quit their jobs. Comments such as "I have

AUGUST

kids to support. Are you going to pay my mortgage while I quit work?" implies that "Either I work or I don't; there is no in-between."

These statements reflect all-or-nothing thinking, an inability to envision the gray areas—a flexible balance between work and leisure or between work and family. It also reflects the driving fear that if you give up your compulsive working, there will be nothing left of your life, and your world will fall apart. These unfounded beliefs can cause you to avoid recovery and to cling more tenaciously to work for security.

The truth is that work/life balance has little to do with work hours or the types of job you're in. It's a different way of thinking about your life—a different way of being on the inside. Rather than limiting your life to work, you become more mindful of integrating it over three other quadrants: relationships with loved ones, play, and self-care. The irony of work/life balance is that it makes you more efficient in your professional and personal lives.

CHASE HAPPINESS INSIDE

Chances are you seek happiness by putting all your eggs into the workbasket, thinking accomplishments, awards, and praise will do the happy trick. But happiness is an inside job. Whether you are happy or not depends on the ways in which you think about day-to-day occurrences. Happiness comes when you can make mindful choices and commit yourself to being happy regardless of what life throws at you.

One of the biggest questions most of us ask is: how do we find happiness? No one knows, because the answer is different for each person. And it doesn't one day walk up and tap you on the shoulder. It takes mindful action on your part. It starts with understanding the ways your mind is set and consciously choosing happiness over misery, no matter what your life conditions happen to be.

RECLAIM SPARE TIME

We all have the same amount of time, and it's finite—168 hours in a week, to be precise. If you subtract your total weekly activity hours from this number, you get the number of hours left over that aren't allotted to work, sleep, or other necessary acts. How can you distribute the remaining hours and best utilize this spare time?

Reclaim your spare time by scheduling an appointment with yourself—just as you would with a colleague at work. When you carve out that blank space in your schedule, you are choosing to make free time a priority. This gives you a block of time leftover each week

#CHILL

to do the hundred other things you would like to do—relax, exercise, decompress from the day, chat with loved ones, meditate, practice yoga, or just watch the sun set.

PONDER SACRED WORK

You become the god you worship. If work addiction is your idol, you become it. Have you thought about the impact your work has beyond your own need to keep doing it? Once you become mindful of the spiritual/helping possibilities of your work, it uplifts you out of the meaningless boredom of daily routines.

Whether you're a plumber, physician, or pilot, ask if your work springs from who you are. Does it bear a relationship to your unfolding journey? Is it holy, sacred, and uplifting? Think about the spiritual/helping components of your daily job tasks. Take a few minutes now to consider the importance of your tasks in terms of a higher purpose. Then contemplate the possibilities of the sacred impact your work has on the ones you serve.

LIVE WITH ABANDON

When was the last time you let go with abandon—danced in front of your bedroom mirror, sang karaoke in your car at the top of your lungs, or skipped down the street like nobody was watching? Has it been a month? A year? A decade? And if so, why? What keeps you from being silly and goofy by yourself and with the ones you love?

What are you afraid of? Living with abandon is a great antidote to overworking. So what are you waiting for? Go ahead. Stop putting limits on yourself. Be outrageous. Sing your heart out. Dance around the house. Skip down the street. Let yourself be silly!

PERSEVERE

The work world can be brutal—full of meteoric challenges, constant negativity, and devastating letdowns. On the days when hopelessness sets in, the key to success is perseverance. You can focus on the obstacles, or you can learn to scale the wall.

Perseverance is the cornerstone of success in anything you try, and only the persistent survive. If you get up and brush yourself off just one more time than you fall, you boost the chances of reaching your work goals. And you land at the finish line with confidence, courage, and calm.

LOVE

A Harvard study, conducted over seventy-five years, found that you can have all the money you want, but without loving relationships, you can't be happy. It's not about the number of relationships you have, but the depth and vulnerability of a quality relationship.

Typically, workaholics put intimate relationships at the bottom of the totem pole. Does this sound like you? If so, perhaps you play your cards close to the chest when it comes to sharing feelings or making yourself vulnerable to others. Instead of being open to giving and receiving love, maybe you place deadlines, work pressures, and task completion in the way. While this protects you from fear of intimacy, it also pushes people away and imprisons you in a lonely sentence of solitary confinement.

Are you remembering to choose love? The next time you consider working late at the office or going into the office on a Saturday instead of hanging out with a friend, child, or spouse, consider chilling and making a happier and healthier choice.

CELEBRATE GOOD TIMES

It's essential to remember to underscore festive occasions that mark your path in life. Celebrations give you time to step back and breathe meaning into your life. Remember that once missed, those special events are gone forever. Looking back, you will regret that you missed your child's first soccer game for a meeting you now don't remember.

Contemplate the important ceremonies and observances that you usually work through. Ask yourself if it's worth investing the time to enjoy them now so you have the memories stored to reflect upon later in life. What's most important to remember? The day you spent working? Or time you spent with loved ones?

ESTABLISH BOUNDARIES

All of us need boundaries for successful work/life integration. Boundary lines keep you safe and healthy. They sustain your individuality and help you establish healthy relationships. They make the lines between work and personal time clear so that you limit work hours to have time for other things. And they enable you to say no when you're already overloaded.

Blurred lines can help with work/life balance as long as it's the work lines that get blurred. The boundaries you set depend upon your unique lifestyle. Some of us, for example, limit work to eight hours a day with no weekend or holiday toil. And some of us who work weekends must figure out how to draw those lines on other days and times. The key to work/life balance is to know when to set boundaries—and when to blur

AUGUST

them. What are some ways you can practice better boundaries in your work life?

LIVE UNCHAINED

Wouldn't it be awesome if you could stay calm and confident in the face of tumultuous challenges, major disappointments, and bludgeoning rejections? How wonderful would it be if you could leave all thoughts of work behind at the office, could be in the present moment with yourself, friends, and loved ones, and could experience every minute outside the office fully without job stress?

Good news! You can get free by connecting with your True Self and living in the present. Try to meditate on mindful ways you can free yourself from oppositional self-talk that chains you to the desk when you're away from the office.

REFRAIN FROM SAVORING YOUR WORK

Ever wonder why a chilled coworker can accomplish more in a day than some workaholics do in a week? Savoring Workaholics are slow, deliberate, and methodical. Consummate perfectionists, they are terrified deep down that the finished product will never be good enough. Dotting every *i* and crossing every *t*, they take eight hours to accomplish a task that a chilled worker could finish in an hour. And they mindlessly prolong work when almost finished with a task, making it difficult to function on a team. Savoring Workaholics get an A-plus on keeping their nose to the grindstone but an F on time management and task completion.

What about you? Do you work harder and longer? Or do you work smarter? Ask yourself if you delegate, prioritize, and know when to release a finished project. Do you manage time so that you're productive, efficient, and capable of working as a team? What can you do to work smarter so you have more time after hours to enjoy your life fully?

MAKE YOUR LIST AND CHECK IT TWICE

Overworking leads to family neglect, insensitivity to the needs of others, suppression of love from those you care about, rejection of anyone who cannot meet your high standards, or belittlement of people who don't conduct business or bake bread as fast or in the exact way you do.

First admit your past mistakes and your self-righteous actions without self-judgment and commit to changing them. Then follow Step 8 of Workaholics

AUGUST

Anonymous, which says to make a list of all persons you have harmed with your abusive work habits and develop a willingness to make amends to them all. As you make your list, be sure to forgive yourself for inflicting self-abuse in the throes of your addiction.

AUGUST TAKEAWAYS

- Become mindful of how you choose words to heal instead of harm.

- Swallow your pride and embrace imperfection.

- Learn to experience your job as a higher purpose and perform it with compassion and devotion.

- Make a list of people your overworking harmed and contemplate a willingness to make amends to each one.

- Celebrate with people you love and live and work with and consider their feelings and opinions.

- Scale the wall of obstacles and persevere by getting up one more time than you fall.

- Develop courage to enter the unknown zone and experience your life with more abandon.

SEPTEMBER

It is very easy to forgive others their mistakes; it takes more grit and gumption to forgive them for having witnessed your own.

—JESSAMYN WEST

APOLOGIZE AND FORGIVE

September is derived from the Latin root *septem,* meaning seven. In the original Roman calendar, September was the seventh month of the year. It became the ninth month when January and February were squeezed in but retained its original meaning of seven.

Some people swear that seven is the luckiest number. After all, there are seven days of the week, seven colors of the rainbow, seven notes on a musical scale, seven seas, and seven continents. Plus the Jewish menorah has seven branches, and Snow White had seven dwarfs. Since September means "seven," it could be the month for you to have a stroke of luck. This is ironic given the fact that September, the ninth month, corresponds to the toughest, most dreaded, and scariest challenge of all. You put the pedal to the metal to make up for lost time and apologize to those you hurt in the throes of overworking, forgive them, ask to be forgiven, and forgive yourself. In terms of the chill factor, this is the month for you to wipe the slate clean by rectifying past hurts so you can move on with greater work/life balance.

Raise your hand if you've carried regrets about

#CHILL

someone you hurt in the past but have done nothing about it. Yep, that's what I thought. Most of you. I can almost see your jaw drop as butterflies flutter in your stomach at the thought of taking this action. I get it, but the risk is worth the effort. Harboring regret keeps it at the center of your daily activities, depletes your energy, and keeps you focused in a negative direction. Offering and accepting forgiveness redeems you from your past. In the aftermath of making amends, you're left with an incredible unburdening of past transgressions that is replaced with deep serenity and peace of mind.

In this chapter, you can ask what you need to do to clean up your life with Right Action—the Buddhist term for ethical conduct in which you do no harm to others, right your wrongs, and cultivate wholeness in yourself. What wounds in your personal history need healing? What action could you take to mend the injury? To whom do you need to say "I'm sorry," apologize, or make amends? And what shame, worry, or guilt do you need to free yourself from by asking forgiveness for being a pain in the ass, speaking badly about someone behind their back, or not being there when a loved one needed you?

You won't be able to track down everyone you hurt in your lifetime. But in tribute to those you cannot make amends to, consider committing to a future of emotional risk taking. Stretch yourself by taking a different action than you would normally take. Feel the fear and do it anyway and enjoy the payoff of self-integration and self-growth. Your ability to stretch into facing past regrets with lovingkindness, compassion, and forgiveness, without judging them as scary or dreadful, is the cornerstone of work/life balance.

If you're willing to look for the opportunity in the fear instead of the fear in the opportunity of making amends, you could hit the jackpot. September could be your big chill, your luckiest month ever. Now is the time to ask if you're willing to take an emotional risk and throw the dice. Otherwise, how will you ever know what magic, wonder, and joy might lie beyond your hesitation?

WEED YOUR GARDEN

Do you treat important relationships like an afterthought, cold leftovers from yesterday's meal, or an old pair of worn shoes you put on for comfort? Do relationships feel more like work after a day of compulsive overworking?

Think of your special bonds as an enchanted garden bursting with beautiful flowers, rose bushes,

SEPTEMBER

CHILL

and ripened fruit trees and vegetables. A healthy garden requires regular maintenance throughout the growing season. Ask yourself if your garden is thriving or dying on the vine from neglect. Just as a garden requires periodic care to grow—weeding, water, sunlight, and fertilizer—relationships need attention, support, compassion, heart-to-heart talks, encouragement, and forgiveness. Nurturing, mindful interactions offset the neglect—demands, avoidance, stress, blame, disagreements, or criticism—that naturally occur in relationships. It's good maintenance to ask if you've tended your relationships each day. Making time to weed your garden gives you a juicy return on the blood, sweat, and tears you put into it.

DON'T LET YOUR BALANCE GET SNATCHED

Watch out. They're everywhere: the balance snatchers that invade your life, creating work addiction, debilitating you, and making you less efficient in your job. Are you stretching workdays into the wee hours to juggle more tasks, taking work home, leashing yourself to devices that make you available to the workplace 24/7? Living this way keeps your natural defenses on red alert, filled with constant doses of adrenaline and cortisol, clobbering you with mental and physical fatigue, and turning you into a more disgruntled, less effective worker.

Even if you're not a workaholic, chances are you have trouble finding work/life balance. A team of Canadian and American researchers found that nearly half of U.S. workers take work home with them and that many of them say work interferes with family, social, and leisure aspects of their lives.

Meditate for a few minutes on some balance snatchers that have invaded your life. After meditation, make a list of the snatchers and the damage they left. Then beside each one name some tried-and-true ways to set boundaries and check the ones you can apply to bring you greater work/life balance.

PRACTICE COMPASSION

Imagine having dinner with someone special in an expensive restaurant. You've looked forward to a quiet evening of candlelight, soft music, and intimate conversation. But your server is impatient and curt. How would you feel? Most people would say annoyed or angry. But then a friend seated at another table comes over to inform you that the server's son was killed in a car wreck and she's a single mom and has to work. Now how would you feel? Most people would say sad, sorry, or empathetic.

SEPTEMBER

CHILL

What happened? How can emotions swing from anger one second to compassion the next? The server didn't change. Your perspective changed now that you see more of the server's inner struggles. Without your friend's insight, odds are you would continue to be annoyed.

It's not always possible to know what wars are waged deep within other people. But we can imagine that most of us have an inside struggle much of the time. Compassion enables us to walk in someone else's shoes and feel the misery or pain they are going through. When we let openheartedness, instead of judgment, lead our behavior, we automatically give other people the benefit of the doubt.

SAY NO TO NAYSAYERS

How many of us are naysayers who gave up because of that negative voice in our heads? Or how many of us gave up because we listened to other naysayers? If you fall into either category, it's time to tune in to your own confidence.

When you heed the advice of the naysayer message, it deafens you to success. Whether you're aiming for work/life balance, a need to chill, or reasonable goals in the workplace, that negative voice can impede your goals. But don't surrender your hopes and dreams to the gloomy limitations that naysayers place on them-selves. Your destiny resides within you, not inside the negative views of others or the negative voice in your head.

LIVE WHOLEHEARTEDLY

Wholehearted living isn't about perfection. It's about imperfection, yet doing your best. It's about allow-ing yourself to be vulnerable and afraid sometimes while at the same time knowing you're courageous. Eight "C-words" complete the list for living in a whole-hearted way:

COURAGE to let uncertain situations happen without knowing the outcomes

COMPASSION for yourself and other human beings, re-gardless of the circumstances

CONNECTEDNESS with others—coworkers, loved ones, and yourself

CLARITY to give you direction to achieve work/life balance

CALMNESS and the loss of the ability to worry about the past or future

#CHILL

CURIOSITY with less interest in judging your coworkers or yourself

CONFIDENCE in your actions instead of acting from past hurts or future fears

CREATIVITY and the ability to flow with ideas and feel bursts of unrestrained joy

Which of the eight C-words could you give more attention to round out a wholehearted life for yourself? If you catch yourself judging a mistake or failure, replace the self-judgment with one of the C-words and notice what happens inside.

COMPLETE IT WITHOUT URGENCY

Chances are you believe everything must be completed today—an impossible goal if applied on a regular basis. Work completion can outweigh the quality of the outcome. Once you take an objective look at your to-do list, your self-imposed unrealistic expectations are obvious. And you learn that few work tasks actually have to be completed immediately. Your flawed perception keeps you in relentless high gear, rushing to finish a self-imposed deadline.

Important things take time. Plants don't rush. They take their time to grow. The seasons change slowly. The Grand Canyon developed over thousands of years. As you remind yourself that important things take time, you allow a natural undisturbed rhythm to determine when work tasks must be finalized. Then you slow down and relax your urgency.

SELF-SOOTHE

You wouldn't dream of talking to a loved one—even a colleague—the way you talk to yourself: "Get a grip" or "Stop feeling sorry for yourself." Harsh words can be more stressful than the outside stressor itself.

Words have power. Under duress, a self-soothing voice helps you cope after big disappointments such as a job loss, missed deadline, or overlooked promotion. Pep talks and affirmations are beneficial during high-pressured situations such as job interviews, speaking in front of peers, or competing for a project.

Do you kick yourself while you're down with oppressive self-talk? Make it a point to speak to yourself in kind, nurturing ways. As you begin to treat yourself with the same lovingkindness and consideration you give to others, you notice a boost in your confidence, resilience, and well-being. Kindness is the language that the deaf can hear and the blind can see. As you

SEPTEMBER

CHILL

soothe yourself from the inside out, you receive more support from the outside in and have more moments of chill time.

THINK AHEAD

Some fast trackers make snap decisions or look for a quick fix because they're in a rush to get as much done as possible. Are you like pieces of popcorn on a hot plate, jumping at the heat's command? Do you launch projects before all facts are gathered and all options are on the table? Or do you underestimate how long a job will take and hurry to complete it? If you bypass research and forethought, you probably make avoidable mistakes and spend more time cleaning up your mess because you didn't think things through.

A little forethought saves you trouble down the road. It helps you set goals and figure out how you can arrive at them. Otherwise, if you don't know where you're going, how do you know where you'll end up? Mindful preparation gives you a more direct path than mindless floundering and more chill time in the long run.

Part of living in the present includes thinking ahead to the future. You can live only for today and still plan for tomorrow. Contemplate on your use of forethought. Then ask how mindful you would say you are in setting goals and planning before moving ahead.

SMILE

It may sound too simple to be true, but science backs it up. You can change your mood by altering your facial expressions. When you frown, you feel bad not simply because it *reflects* how you feel, but also, the facial expression *contributes* to how you feel.

The same is true with smiling. It makes you feel happier. Even if you fake it, pasting a smile on your face can raise your mood and reduce stress. Plus, coworkers and family members respond to you in a more uplifting way. Studies show that facial expressions influence your emotions by triggering specific neurotransmitters, the brain's chemical messengers. When people whose ability to frown is compromised by cosmetic Botox injections, they're happier than people who can frown.

So next time you're feeling bad, remember that frowning makes you feel worse. But you can jump-start a feel-good workday by putting on a happy face and smiling. Even if you have to fake it to start, smiling reduces your stress, elevates your mood, and creates a positive impact on your coworkers.

MEDITATE ON IMPERMANENCE

When you stop to think about it, everything is impermanent. Every material thing you own will erode,

SEPTEMBER

#CHILL

break, or decay. And you will eventually die. Contemplating on impermanence can help you think more mindfully of how you want to spend today. What's important to complete? Who do you want to spend time with? How do you want to spend it?

Asking yourself these questions reminds you that tomorrow brings no guarantees and underscores the importance of living each precious moment to the fullest. Perhaps it can help you appreciate the people and things before your eyes that hurry and harriedness have taken you away from.

Think about what you have overlooked or taken for granted while rushing to the next item on your agenda. Then meditate on what it would be like if you lived today extraordinarily, as though it were your last.

CALIBRATE YOUR STRESS NEEDLE

It isn't stress that kills you, it's your reaction to it. When you constantly react to stressors, you swim in your own cortisol and adrenaline stew that harms your body.

One way to regulate stress and to get a clear picture of how it changes over time is to map it with what I call the stress needle. Ask yourself how stressed you feel on a 10-point scale, with 0 being not stressed at all and 10 being so stressed you could explode.

Your stress needle might be at a 3 (0–3, no stress) right now after a high-pressure presentation, but it was a 7 or 8 last month when you had that big job interview. When you realize your needle is moderate (4–7) to high (8–10), have your toolbox ready to lower the needle with simple stress management strategies that will reduce it: deep breathing, meditation, exercise, or yoga. Compare your response to different situations and see if you can figure out which stressors trigger you the most.

FOLLOW THE TEN COMMANDMENTS OF SELF-CARE

Work/life balance can be a game changer when you follow my Ten Commandments of Self-Care. As you read down the list, ask yourself which ones you practice and which ones you need to start to follow.

1. Thou shalt get regular exercise, eat healthy, and get plenty of rest and sleep.
2. Thou shalt muster the courage to laugh and play a quarter of your time.
3. Thou shalt practice mindful, present-moment awareness at work, home, and play.
4. Thou shalt treat yourself with great respect and compassion.

SEPTEMBER

5. Thou shalt deepen your connection to loved ones, friends, and yourself.

6. Thou shalt expand your interests and talents beyond your daily work role.

7. Thou shalt keep a positive and confident outlook at all times.

8. Thou shalt cultivate more curiosity than judgment into the roots of your work addiction.

9. Thou shalt practice mindfulness meditation and contemplation to maintain inner calm and clarity on a regular basis.

10. Thou shalt abstain from excessive work and create work/life balance in all your affairs.

PUT A STOP TO THE SHIT STORMS

Many of us grew up in homes where conflict occurred on a regular basis. Chaos feels normal, and we become addicted to risk and excitement. We're drawn to high-pressured jobs, create crisis in the workplace, and get an adrenaline rush by overworking to put out the fire we set.

Is your life one shit storm after another? If so, perhaps you pack your life so full you don't leave space for life's random events. You overschedule, put too many irons in the fire, set unrealistic deadlines, or refuse to punch out at a reasonable time. Sometimes it's difficult for you to see the water you swim in, and you cannot see how you're creating your own hardships. Just because your world seems to fall apart doesn't mean you have to. Your life becomes unmanageable when you try to run it without keen introspection and an objective eye.

Without judgment, start to pay attention to your attraction to chaos. Ask, "What do I gain from the drama?" and contemplate the answers. Comfort? Success? Control? Importance? Once you discover the roots, try to find more constructive ways to cushion unexpected events and avoid exhaustion so you can attain satisfaction in the workplace and your personal life.

FEUD LESS

Feuds are like poisons. When you stubbornly continue to oppose others, you shut off the dark corners of your spirit from the healing you need. When you tell and retell your stories laden with blame, anger, and the unfairness of what someone did to you, you fill those dark corners. Harboring feuds on the inside eats away at you until you're consumed by the cortisol-adrenaline soup that eventually drowns you.

If you survey your inner emotional landscape, how many people do you feud with? Yourself for not doing enough? Your kids for not measuring up? Your co-worker for not getting it right? How important are the feuds? And what toxic feelings do you hold on to that need to be released?

Meditate on resolving the feuds, and commit to stop feeding the darker corners of your soul. Consider turning the feuds into love and forgiveness in order to unblock your path to recovery.

DECLARE YOUR WORTH

Many overachievers believe you must earn the right to be—that you have no value unless you're producing something of value. Your shame and self-loathing won't allow you simply to work an average amount. To be legitimate, you think you must overcompensate and do more than the average person. You turn yourself into a human doer instead of a human being. The more you produce, the better you are because the more worthy you feel.

You earned the right to be the day you were born. You no longer have to go beyond and above what other people do to feel okay. You can either spend your life slaving under these unrealistic standards or concentrate on respecting yourself as you are.

Take a few minutes to reflect on the idea that the right to be is your birthright. Then contemplate on what your work habits would look like if you practiced this belief on a daily basis.

DON'T BE A WET FALLEN LEAF

Japanese wives use the derogatory term *nure-ochiba* (a wet fallen leaf that sticks annoyingly to the leg) to refer to retired workaholic husbands who don't know what to do with themselves once they're not working and hang around the house expecting their wives to plan their spare time.

Many Americans also say their workaholic spouses seem lost and helpless during downtimes such as vacations, holidays, or retirement. After working from dawn to dusk for so many years, you start to feel like a fringe family dweller. You develop the habit of opting out of family chores and outings, making yourself marginal. If you wait too long to engage, it can be too late. Family members solidify internal alliances and develop their routines. After years of absence, loved ones rebuff your attempts to become actively involved. Your displacement, in turn, triggers a need for connection with your old friend: work. And the cycle continues.

Contemplate some mindfulness actions you can

SEPTEMBER

take within your family so you don't become a wet fallen leaf.

STOP CLINGING TO MISERY

Control is one of the hallmarks of workaholism. When you insist that everything meets your specifications, you create suffering for yourself. As an example, a passenger who missed his connection at the Charlotte International Airport threw a fit with the airline until they informed him that the plane he missed crashed and no one on board survived. Needless to say, the passenger fell to his knees in gratitude.

Clinging to certainty causes misery, but you don't have to stay stuck there. The way out of suffering is to step back from your predicaments. When things don't work out to suit, you can watch with curiosity how your will wants to react without reacting. Remind yourself that your visions are based on limited knowledge—that things happen beyond your understanding and that life can actually take you to heights of satisfaction that you never imagined.

Meditate on expanding your outlook and finding room for more than your ego expects. This exercise, if practiced on a regular basis, reduces suffering and cultivates the life you're meant to have instead of the life you plan to have.

DECIDE YOUR OWN MOOD

Those of us who work for an organization toil under the expectations of our employers. Over time, this can create boredom, frustration, even resentment. But what about your daily moods and goals?

After all, studies show that morning moods stay with you all day. So as you prepare to start your day, remember you can personalize your work and feel more empowered in the process. Perhaps the boss wants you to cold-call a certain number of clients each day. How about you meet that goal with the added personal goal of looking for one positive thing about each client you meet?

When you set reachable goals around themes of confidence, calm, and positivity, you weave personal actions into reactions to the company's requests. You make your private goals a priority so they don't get lost under the pile of tasks. You focus back on your goals throughout the day to ensure you have the momentum to keep pursuing them. At day's end, even if you didn't achieve the company's goal, you can savor the satisfaction of having accomplished your own.

UTILIZE YOUR CREATIVE INSTINCTS

In order to exercise your creative instincts at work, you need an open mind that allows you to consider

SEPTEMBER

limitless possibilities to think outside the box. Creative instincts release you from the grip of the rational mind where your inner critic resides and immerses you into an intuitive wisdom of another kind—a wisdom that helps you see and make healthy, productive decisions from an entirely different place in a totally different way.

Creativity goes hand in hand with clear-mindedness and the courage to risk letting go. It fosters being synchronized with the ebb and flow of life, a creative harmony that manifests as peak moments, oneness, and a rich sense of being fully alive. When you exercise your creative instincts, you don't push the river, because you're flowing in the moment.

Wonder what it would be like if each workday were involving, fun, and creative? Contemplate some mindfulness actions you can take to participate more fully in the creative process. Then commit yourself to when and where you might implement these new ideas.

TAKE CARE OF YOURSELF

From time to time, you may find yourself putting your needs at the bottom of the list in order to take care of others. You even may be attracted to friends, loved ones, and business associates for whom you feel sorry and who need help. Rescuing keeps the focus off you and on someone else. You may hear a lecture and think, "Now this is what my spouse or friend needs to hear," instead of absorbing the advice for yourself.

Self-sacrifice is a virtue, so we are told, and putting yourself last shows strength of character. Truth be told, if you want to help others, the key is to take care of yourself first from a place of strength, not weakness. When you sacrifice your well-being (nutrition, rest, and exercise), you become overly stressed and burnt out, which limits the amount of energy you can give to your job, loved ones, and friends. When you're already overloaded, the key is self-care—to do things that interest and replenish you.

If a colleague asks you to do something you don't want to do, say no. Speak up when a friend takes advantage of your good nature. Refuse to bail a loved one out of trouble for the umpteenth time. Sometimes the best way to care is drawing a line that protects you. Self-care prepares you to give more love and nurturance to others. When you put yourself first, there is more of you to go around.

ASK FOR FORGIVENESS

Past mistakes can never be fully erased, but they can be mended. The purpose of Step 9 of Workaholics Anonymous is restitution and reconciliation. You take

SEPTEMBER

action and make direct amends to those you harmed with nonstop working. This Step has the potential to provide you with peace of mind and liberation from the chain of regret. When you make amends, you ask for forgiveness out of humility and genuine desire, not out of guilt or obligation. During the amendment process, you suddenly realize that the little child inside you has grown up and that you're a more mature, responsible adult. You have restored your self-respect and the respect of others.

Learning to forgive is a true measure of successful recovery. And it's important to extend forgiveness for the abuse to yourself in the mix. As long as you can forgive, you will never be defeated. Ask whom you have hurt with your work abuse and to whom you need to make amends. Then make direct amends to those people unless it would harm them and then extend that same forgiveness to yourself.

SEPTEMBER TAKEAWAYS

- Identify the balance snatchers and don't let them invade your life.

- Apply the eight C's for self-integration and to achieve wholehearted living.

- Refuse to pressure yourself with unreasonable deadlines.

- Jump-start your workday by smiling even if you have to fake it before it feels real.

- Put yourself into the present moment while being mindful of impermanence.

- Follow the Ten Commandments of Self-Care to cultivate greater work/life integration.

- Commit to active family participation instead of hanging out on the sidelines.

- Apologize to people you hurt, ask for forgiveness, and forgive the ones who hurt you.

OCTOBER

As soon as we come
up against the least
edge of pain, we're going
to run; we'll never know
what's beyond that
particular barrier or
wall or fearful thing.

—PEMA CHÔDRÔN

CONTINUITY AND THE NEW NORMAL

In October the days are abundant with colorful, falling leaves. Orange pumpkins dot the landscape. The days start to get shorter. And there's a chill in the air that matches the chill you have now cultivated on the inside. You celebrate the changing seasons with Oktoberfest or Halloween. This month's theme is sustaining the new normal that you have developed to deal with your old ways.

Your colleagues leave the office at a reasonable time. They take their families on vacation. They attend their children's school activities. And they're as productive and successful as you are. What's wrong with this picture? By now, you know your mind plays tricks on you. It distorts your thoughts in ways you were not aware of before.

In this chapter, you commit to ongoing mindfulness practices that you have established to keep your life on even keel. You're continually willing to let go of negativity, control, anger, and all the other habits that previously caused your life to go into the crapper. You continue to take a personal inventory and when wrong promptly admit it, determined not to relapse into old workaholic habits.

#CHILL

You're mindful that you're no longer on duty to shoulder the weight of the world. Perhaps you're less attached to outcomes and do your best to accept what happens. Worry, control, and impatience become burdens of the past. You continue to remind yourself what you can change about yourself and what you can't change in others. You don't let small catastrophes of time urgency steal the calm and serenity you've been building. You slow down and chill your frantic work habits and continue to include meditation and mindful eating and drinking to quiet your mind.

Many of the questions remain the same, but you're committed to a different mindset. Will the big honchos shoot down my idea? Can I meet the deadline? Will I make it home in time for dinner? When something bad happens, you become curious, instead of judgmental, and ask, "How can I look at this hardship in a different way and turn it around to benefit me?" Perhaps you think, "My boss doesn't have confidence in me." And you do a turnaround with a more truthful thought: "Maybe I don't believe in myself right now."

You start to suspend your beliefs and stop jumping to conclusions. You no longer hit the ground running, eat on the run, or skip meals to get work done. You refrain from giving the finger to the slow commuter in front of you and from snarling at a coworker for being a slacker. Your habit of magnifying small problems into huge roadblocks and drenching your nervous system with a cocktail of stress, frustration, or impatience becomes a distant memory.

You may not even know it, but the new normal in your outlook and your continued actions change the structure of your brain over time. You rewire your brain with automatic, healthier patterns that lead you to automatic chill and work/life integration.

SLOW DOWN WITH MEDITATION

Mindfulness meditation quiets the mind. It does what the medicine field once relied on drugs to do: slows down heart rate and brain wave patterns and boosts the immune system. The following present-moment meditation can help you pay closer attention to the needs of your body, mind, and spirit.

Visualize yourself going through your day moment to moment at a slow pace. Start with awakening. Take yourself through your daily routine while slowing down. See yourself showering, eating, and driving slower, staying in the now and doing one task at a time. See the events of the day as they unfold. Release any urges to

OCTOBER

#CHILL

hurry. Notice how you feel as you chill in the present. As you pay close attention to your body, notice what it needs that it hasn't been getting. What does your mind need? Visualize yourself attending to those needs one by one. Repeat this exercise as often as needed.

CHANGE YOURSELF FIRST

By now it comes as no big surprise that workaholics are notorious for the unhealthy need to control other people and situations. That's why you love work; you can control it. Or at least you fool yourself into thinking you can.

Truth be told, it's hard enough to change yourself, much less trying to change someone else. Think of it as two sides of the street. Beyond what you think, feel, and the actions you take, there's little you can change. The more focused you are on keeping your own side of the street clean, the more manageable your life becomes.

When you're mindful of how often you try to change another person—in small and big ways—you might be surprised how often you inflict this control onto co-workers, friends, and family. These actions are futile and stressful and add another layer of "work" on top of the job you do on a daily basis. Ask yourself what you're resisting that creates unnecessary stress. And what do you need to let go of that you can't change so you have more serenity in your life?

SAY THANK YOU TO YOUR POSSE

Few of us can take full credit for our achievements, although much of the time we fail to recognize those who helped us. Chances are you have a posse of loved ones, friends, and coworkers who helped you to get where you are—some obvious, some more subtle. Perhaps a spouse or friend handled family outings or financial responsibilities, standing in the background, holding you up while you toiled around the clock. Maybe a parent helped out or a neighbor. Or maybe you were fortunate enough to have outside hired help to keep your personal life afloat.

There are many ways to say thank you to the ones who have your back: a kind deed, a special dinner, or taking time for heart-to-heart talks. Even a handwritten card shows appreciation. Consider everyone who helped you along the way. How are you thanking them for their support? How do you want to do so moving forward?

OCTOBER

BE ASSERTIVE, NOT AGGRESSIVE

Conflicting interests and disagreements are natural in the workplace, but you can work out your differences without being adversarial. After all, you want to sell your ideas to colleagues and clients without steamrolling, criticizing, or finger-pointing.

There are times, though, when you must confront someone at work. The best approach is the path of assertiveness—not the extremes of aggression or passivity. You are an active listener, engage in what a colleague has to say, and remain open to other ideas that conflict with your own. Instead of being defensive, you're kind, considerate, and respectful—yet firm and clear in stating your perspectives.

How do you think you measure up on this middle path? What are some aspects to your approach you could change?

ROCK OUT

If you put little rocks in a jar before trying to fit the big rocks, there won't be room for the larger ones. But if you put the big rocks in first, the small ones fall in around them. Some things are more important than others. If you consider what's most important, you're likely to be more successful with work/life balance. It's important to be mindful of which aspects of your life are key. Set clear and practical priorities. Wrap your priorities around the people you love, not the people you love around your work.

What are your big rocks? What do you wrap your life around?

LET DOWN YOUR DEFENSE

We all are defensive or hotheaded at times. You're wired for it, so it doesn't make you a bad person when you feel that way. Someone angers or hurts you and a wall goes up automatically. It's the elegant design of your nervous system.

You need defenses against threats for survival just as you need your rib cage to protect your vital organs. But truth be told, few of us encounter threats on a regular basis. Yet your defenses respond as if you're under attack when you're threatened with a spouse leaving, loss of a promotion, or a child having trouble in school.

Suppose you were to become mindful of dropping your defenses and opening yourself to new experiences. What if you asked, "What am I defending within myself?" and "What would each moment be like if I were mindfully open to life without defenses?"

Wonder what your world would be like if you were free, chilled, and unafraid of each day as it unfolds?

OCTOBER

SAY YES MORE

Chances are you automatically say no more than yes—especially to requests that might interfere with work. Over time, the accumulation of a thousand little nos can create a closed-off life. A few yesses can add up, opening a whole universe of life-changing experiences.

Try this experiment for one day: pay attention to how many requests, opportunities, invitations, or questions you say no to. It can be a party invitation, drinks after work with coworkers, dinner with friends, attending a family reunion.

Note in your phone every time you say no. At the end of the day, tally the number of times you turned down something because of work. How many nos could be a new chance to grow or make new friends? Wonder how many times you missed out on the life you were supposed to have because you held too tightly to the life you thought you were supposed to have? Perhaps your holding back is the one suffering you could have avoided.

DON'T BE A WORK ABUSER

Are you the type of worker who works more than forty or fifty hours a week, skipping lunch breaks to eat at your desk, staying in constant contact with the office on weekends, holidays, and vacations, feeling nervous or antsy when away from the office?

If you're a work abuser, you use your job to escape from personal problems. Work is a place where life really happens for you—the secret repository of drama and emotion—a place of safety from life's unpredictability at a distance from unwanted feelings or commitments. When you abuse work to escape an unpleasant state, you're really interested in hiding out, which ironically creates more stress than the things you are trying to escape.

If you're a work user, you know when to set limits. You're fully present with family and friends and *use* work as a necessary and fulfilling obligation. If you're a workaholic, you *abuse* work in a desperate attempt to escape from something you're unable to face.

Where do you fall on the spectrum of work use and abuse? Have you avoided facing anything that needs attention?

ADJUST YOUR ATTITUDE

When I first set foot in Venice, I was dazzled by the aroma and flavor of Italian food, the architecture of the ancient buildings, and the romantic gondolas

OCTOBER

CHILL

floating in the canals to the sounds of old-world music. By the end of the vacation, I noticed cracks in the pavement, the hot, dusty air, garbage floating in the canals, and graffiti that marred the buildings. Venice was still the same romantic, beautiful place as when I arrived, but in my mind it had soured. When I realized that my attitude—not the city—had changed, I was able to revert to my original impression.

When left to its own devices, your attitude can slide you into negativity and self-defeat. See if you can think of an attitude that you need to adjust. Practice shifting your attitude about a person, place, or situation once or twice a day until positive feelings increase and stress symptoms subside.

DO IT OVER

When faced with mortality, you pay closer attention to how you're leading your life. Suddenly you want to live differently, and life becomes more meaningful. I thought about what I'd do differently if I could have a do-over.

I'd slow down, work less, and play more. I'd leave my bed unmade in the morning and instead watch the sunrise and birds at the bird feeder. I'd forget about perfection. I'd speak my truth—even if it hurt someone's feelings. I'd spend less time on social media and more time in heart-to-heart talks with friends and loved ones. I'd have more devil-may-care moments, cast my fate to the wind, stick my neck out, and sing carpool karaoke like nobody's watching. I'd walk barefoot in a rain shower without an umbrella. I'd take a wellness day from work, instead of a sick day, and not worry that the world would go into a holding pattern. I'd hold my spouse in bed instead of my laptop. I'd realize that my work is important but not as much as all the things I missed along the way. What about you? Make a list of some of the things you would do differently if you had a do-over.

NOTICE HOW FAR YOU'VE PROGRESSED

Whether it's working on a relationship, saving money, losing weight, or completing a project, if you're harried and hurried you probably skip the intermediate stages because that's when you get disheartened. It's natural to grow impatient on the way to your goals. When you're feeling lost and hopeless, knowing that progress is composed of the stages of inability, uncertainty, and doubt can boost your confidence to keep paddling. Midway is where progress seems to slow down. You grow impatient and give up on your goals because you see how far you still have to go but forget to look at how far you've come.

OCTOBER

Progress is gradual and occurs in unseen degrees. Small steps slowly mount up, just as brooks become rivers and rivers run into seas. The recognition of how far you've come—not just reaching the goal—gives a truer picture of your progress. You acknowledge the five pounds you lost rather than focusing on the stubborn ten that hang on. If you're trying to improve a relationship, you ask, "Are things better?" not "Are things perfect?"

PUT THE KIBOSH ON FAULT-FINDING MISSIONS

How often do you find yourself on a fault-finding mission with others—even with yourself? It's almost as if you're looking for excuses to be frustrated or angry, determined to pin someone against the wall with their mistakes and incompetence. Do you feel more secure or in control when colleagues face defeat? Do you feel more competent the more inept a coworker looks?

It's one thing to get paid for evaluating, assessing, and doling out constructive criticism in your job. It's quite another to exert your superiority over others in a mean-spirited way to disguise your own insecurities. Most of us are doing our best. When you go on a fault-finding mission, it's important to ask what you gain. Power? Self-worth? Revenge? Security?

Your faults are part of your human condition. All of us have them. They make you who you are. If you're a card-carrying fault-finder, consider trading in your card and becoming a bona fide "favor-finder."

CONTINUE TO TAKE STOCK

Step 10 of Workaholics Anonymous says, "We continued to take personal inventory and when we were wrong promptly admitted it." In Step 10 you continue the process begun in Step 4—gaining awareness of your feelings and taking responsibility for your words and actions.

Your highest job is to live a better life. You maintain a climate of honesty and openness at the office, factory, or at home. You get in the habit of cleaning your own side of the street. You admit your wrongs and imperfections without self-condemnation and give up rationalizations, justifications, and alibis for past shortcomings. You use the same yardstick with colleagues or loved ones who make mistakes. You continue to forgive others and yourself and to establish reasonable work schedules and deadlines that reduce stress and improve productivity.

You're mindful that no one arrives at perfection and that life is a series of lessons and mistakes from which to learn. By taking daily stock of where you went wrong and admitting it, you grow healthier and stronger. A lifelong process of self-examination and self-insight keeps you chilled in a topsy-turvy work world.

OCTOBER TAKEAWAYS

- Quiet your mind by meditating for five minutes each day.

- Thank everyone who has supported you while you worked around the clock.

- Be assertive instead of aggressive or passive.

- Contemplate saying yes when you automatically want to say no.

- Let down your defenses when they aren't needed so you can be more open.

- Recognize progress you've made when you want to focus on how far you have to go.

- Whenever you feel like fault-finding, go on a favor-finding mission instead.

- Continue to take stock of your mistakes and wrongdoings and promptly admit it.

NOVEMBER

#Chill isn't something you do—it's a mindset, a way of being in the world.

HEIGHTENED CONSCIOUS CONNECTIONS

November is a transition period from the sunny autumn harvest to the cold of winter. You may not know whether to wear a T-shirt or a warm jacket, but one thing is for sure: you have a heightened awareness of how destructive your old life of rushing and hurrying has become. And once it's out, you can't put the toothpaste back in the tube.

In many ways, November is a sacred month. In the United States, it's the time to celebrate Thanksgiving. You give thanks and express gratitude through mediation or prayer for the abundance in your life. All the other months have brought you to where you are now as a result of your practices. Your rising consciousness gives oxygen to a heightened state of spiritual awareness. Constantly aware of Right Action, you continue to seek heightened conscious contact, and your actions come from your heart, not just from your head. As a result of your mindfulness practices, you are more conscious of the feelings of others and more in tune with your own emotion and inner wisdom. And your changes within are reflected in your changed behaviors.

#CHILL

You spend more quality time with loved ones and friends because you enjoy it. You're patient and courteous to the supermarket cashier whom you ridiculed for being too slow, because you recognize she's doing her best. You acknowledge and compliment coworkers for a job well done because they deserve recognition. You advise friends to slow down and chill because you care about them. You pay attention to your own personal needs because you're worth the attention. You apologize to family members for pushing them too hard because you regret it. You help family members with household chores because it's your responsibility to do your part at home. You attend your child's recital or soccer game because you're as interested in their lives as much as you're interested in your own.

In this chapter, you ask yourself what changes you can still make to cultivate a richer, healthier, and more soulful life. You consider the neglected areas in your life and develop a willingness to step outside your comfort zone. As the direct result of a deeper spiritual consciousness, you start to identify the steps you can take to stretch into a more soulful life. You don't get up in the wee morning hours, hit the ground running, and ask what you can knock out early on. You have distance from task completion and consider the now instead of the end result. You suspend your need to finish tasks and focus on lovingkindness of everything and everyone around you in the present moment. And you hold them in a safe place.

Welcome home.

TRY CHAIR YOGA

When your job is a pain in the neck and you've sat for long periods of time, your body needs attention to keep up with your productive mind. Chair yoga is a gentle form of yoga that helps you chill and enhances mental clarity, physical strength, and flexibility. If you don't have time to get to the gym, you can practice chair yoga between appointments right at your desk.

Sitting in your chair, inhale and raise your arms toward the ceiling. Let your shoulder blades slide down your back as you reach upward with your fingertips. Anchor your sit bones in your seat and reach up from there. Place your left hand over your right knee and right arm on back of the chair. Stretch lightly for sixty seconds. Place your right hand over your left knee with left arm on back of the chair for another sixty seconds.

COW POSE: With both feet on the floor, lengthen your spine. Place you hands on your knees. Inhale and arch

NOVEMBER

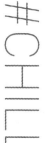

your spine, rolling shoulders back and down. Bring your shoulder blades onto your back.

CAT POSE: Round your spine, dropping your chin to chest allowing the shoulders and head to drop forward. Alternate between the cow pose on the inhalations and the cat pose on the exhalations for five breaths.

HEAL YOUR WORK DYSMORPHIA

Work dysmorphia is a skewed perspective of your work habits, in which your flaws are either imagined or severely exaggerated and your workload is never enough. Perhaps you claim you don't work all that much, and a full workweek is only half-full. On the inside, you feel like a slacker during half workdays, weekends, or vacations.

While you exceed the expectations of others, your perceptions are so rigid and distorted that in your head you never reach your own standards. Under harsh self-judgment, you keep plugging away until you get it right—which you rarely do, and you feel like a failure much of the time. When you set a goal for yourself that you can actually achieve, you think, "That wasn't worth it; that was nothing." Then you create higher goals that you can't possibly attain.

Meditate on some ways you can gain a more balanced perspective on the standards you set for yourself. Ask yourself what actions you can take to heal your skewed view of how long and how often you work compared to how little and infrequently you chill.

BREATHE CONSCIOUSLY

Whether stressors are from work or home, sometimes stress comes at you from all angles. The human body discharges 70 percent of its toxins through breathing. If your breathing isn't operating at peak efficiency, you're not ridding yourself of toxins. Conscious deep breathing puts life back into your body, helps conquer the strains of daily life, and salves your soul.

Notice your breath right now. Is it coming from high in your chest or deep in your abdomen? Is it fast or slow? When you take conscious deep breaths, you can't get as worked up over last-minute deadlines or missed appointments. Breathe deeply throughout the workday because your body can't maintain the same level of stress with the extra oxygen in your bloodstream when you breathe from your abdomen.

GET COMFORTABLE BEING ALONE

Chances are you spend so much time working that you feel cut off from others. Sometimes the only way you can join in a conversation is to talk about work. And

NOVEMBER

#CHILL

eventually that gets old and boring. Wedded to work, you have little time left for interactions with others. You isolate yourself even when you're not working, and you feel like an outsider and forget how to have fun. Your best friend is your laptop, but autocorrect is the only time it talks back.

Seekers who have moments of deep spirituality or authentic relationships with themselves say the main benefit is they don't feel alone. When you take time to have an enduring relationship with yourself, you begin to feel more whole. Plus, there's always a place for you with friends, colleagues, and family members once you stop denying your worth, enjoy interests outside work, and take the time to share them with others.

Ponder how you might have separated yourself from family and friends—even work colleagues who like to have fun around the office. The culprit that isolates you and causes you to feel like an outsider isn't your friends, family, or coworkers. It's the compulsive need to work that usurps the time you could spend with others.

BE RESOURCEFUL

A resource is anything that helps you feel calmer by putting the brakes on the stress response. It can be something you like about yourself, a positive memory or experience, person, place, pet, spiritual guide, or anything that gives you comfort, joy, or serenity.

To activate your resource, simply bring it to mind, along with all the details of it that sustain or nurture you. One of my resources is the memory of sipping morning coffee on the screened porch of a rented beach cottage, watching shrimp boats glide through the water before a huge red-ball sunrise.

Bring your resource to mind in vivid detail. Then direct your attention inside to your internal sensory experience. Note where in your body you feel the pleasing sensations that your resource activates. Pay attention to your breathing, heart rate, and muscle tension. Be mindful of the changes. Your breathing might slow down or your muscles could loosen. Spend a few minutes focusing on whatever changes. As you end the exercise, bring your attention to your whole body, noticing all the changes that occurred and staying with those changes for a few moments.

WITNESS

You probably have war stories about your personal struggles with trying to get it all done: work, family, children, friendships, and, if there's time—yourself. You can get so caught up in past stories that they keep

NOVEMBER

you stuck as the actor in a drama as you replay the hardships over and over in your mind. "Ain't it awful!"

When you put yourself in the position of the one on the receiving end, you continue to feel victimized. But if you put yourself in the position of the witness of an unpleasant situation, it takes you out of the subjective mode and puts you in the role of a dispassionate observer. The role of witness to your previous wounds prevents you from feeling the pain again and has the potential to empower you to move on.

As you hang out on the sidelines with your newly discovered power, try to rewrite the narrative. The event is over and done with. You can remember instead when you knew you were safe or that it was over. You can focus on the people who were there to protect, help, and support you. When you try this, notice how different it feels inside.

ACKNOWLEDGE YOUR INHERENT VALUE

What shifts do you need to make inside so you can engage in work with calmness, confidence, and joy? You can change your view of what the corporate culture and business honchos lead you to believe about work. You're more than just a cog in a machine, more than how you manage time, how much you produce, or how fast you meet deadlines. You're more than your executive expectations, hard decisions, and task completion.

It's time to stop unseeing the truth about yourself. The qualities you bring to work are your inherent value, self-respect, and sacred meaning in everything you do. You don't have to overdo to prove yourself. You're already worthy. You're already valuable. You have everything you need; all you have to do is show up and apply your inherent value.

SAUNTER

I know, I know. It's a paradox, but the more you saunter instead of speed, the more efficient you are. I've found it to be true in my personal life and studies back it up. Remember: the tortoise won the race!

You're probably so used to speeding, you think that that's the only manner in which to get everything done. But rushing clogs your mind, burns you out, and reduces your effectiveness. Going through the workday with ease and stillness, on the other hand, keeps energy up, the mind clear, and productivity high. And by the end of the day you often have reserves leftover.

You don't have to continue to allow constant work pressures to dictate your life. It's possible to make time to do the things you love. While this might sound

NOVEMBER

impossible, it isn't. It's counterintuitive, perhaps, but your body wasn't designed to hurry 24/7. Unless you're under threat, you're designed to saunter so you don't wear out before your time. Spend the rest of the day sauntering to all of your appointments and notice what happens.

THROW IT IN REVERSE

If you're hard-driven, you live your life backward. You spend too much time busily trying to control the outer world, focused on completing tasks and keeping order. You try to gain material things, approval, or money so you can have more of what you want to make you happy.

Balance and chill involve living your life in reverse. You learn to live beyond the illusion of control and to relinquish that control to a Higher Power. The first step is to live from the inside out instead of the outside in by cultivating a rich and healthy internal life. That requires you to first find yourself and be yourself through insight, clarity, and deep contemplation into the roots of your imbalance.

Take some time to ponder what needs correction on the inside before you strive to create your outer life. Can you pinpoint what you've tried to achieve on the outside to fill you up on the inside? Is it possible to identify what you need to do to fill that empty space on the inside before casting your net externally so you can enjoy fully what awaits you?

EMBRACE PAIN

To face pain and suffering as equally as pleasure and happiness contradicts our basic human nature. Yet the truth is, you find happiness by accepting your pain and suffering instead of trying to escape into something more pleasant.

In my own personal growth, adopting this counter-intuitive path continues to be my biggest challenge to some of my old bad habits. Yet I find when I embrace pain and suffering, it releases me from fear, helps me chill, and I feel more calm and compassion. Painful situations can teach you to live beyond the illusion of control. They help you grow and cultivate wisdom. They awaken the courage and resilience you didn't realize exist within you. Pain and suffering transport you from your basic animal instinct of avoidance to a deeper self-understanding, meaningful spiritual connection, and true compassion for others.

What about you? Is it possible to consider facing your pain and suffering instead of running away? Do you trust that this less traveled path might lead you to a deeper connection with others and yourself? As

#CHILL

you meditate on these ideas, see if you discover more calm and compassion and less pain and suffering.

AFFIRM YOUR EFFORTS

Inner dialogue has awesome power. It can make you think you can achieve something or give up before you even try. Even if you have the ability, you might tell yourself you can't. Whether you're starting a new job, pitching an idea to management, or interviewing for a promotion, you can choose which direction your inner dialogue takes. It's just as easy to affirm your abilities with a positive message as it is to tear yourself down.

Positive affirmations help you cope better with adversity because they help you see solutions to work/life problems. They are not tricks to convince you that a situation is better than it actually is. They are prescriptions of encouragement within your reach: "I can do what I set my mind to do" or "I can manage this situation with ease."

You become proficient on a regular basis at what you tell yourself. A positive outlook can undo the damage that stress does to your mind and body. It literally helps repair cardiovascular wear and tear. Positive affirmations send the body a different message than negative emotions, creating a calming effect. Think about what positive support you need to give yourself to change the course of your life.

WRAP YOUR ARMS AROUND FAILURE *AND* SUCCESS

Everything has its opposite. In order to wrap your arms around success, you must first accept its opposite: failure. I realize that might sound crazy, but you can't have a beginning without an end, a front without a back, an up without a down. If you're driving yourself up a wall trying to gain acceptance, you must first accept that gain and loss work in concert.

Perhaps you want your work proposal to be accepted, but can you accept its rejection? You can accept winning the promotion, but can you accept losing it? You want your family to support your work habits, but are you willing to accept that they don't?

Everything has bookends. To attain what you want, you must be willing to accept what you don't want. Choosing acceptance fertilizes your motivation to get up and dust off one more time than you fall. When you loosen your attachment to an outcome, it's easier to accept failure when it comes.

NOVEMBER

#CHILL

BE OPEN TO CONSTRUCTIVE CRITICISM

Since you put so much effort into your job, you are probably overly sensitive to criticism. You don't want to hear even minor constructive criticism. You want praise, the higher the better. But how does that help you grow? Sure, it feels good to be praised, but it's a problem to get caught up in it. If you always search for praise and ignore constructive criticism, you run the risk of being ruined by praise when you could be saved by helpful criticism.

In order to excel, you can be willing to accept constructive feedback from colleagues, friends, and family members. The only way you can know yourself and succeed is through the mirror of human relationships. If your ego is too fragile to appreciate constructive criticism, then you might as well surround yourself with pets—because they can't talk back.

Truth be told, you can't always see the water you're swimming in. Some criticism can save you from drowning. When you make this attitude adjustment, like good medicine, it makes a bitter pill go down.

Can you handle constructive criticism without taking it personally? Can you listen with a dispassionate ear and regard it as helpful? If not, what do you need to change to understand that there could be something wrong with what you did, not something wrong with you?

AVOID DRUMMING YOUR FINGERS

Time is a precious commodity for most of us. You, too, right? You don't like to be kept waiting. You're not accustomed to lulls between tasks. In the age of "instant everything," your driven personality can find long lead times and the glacial pace of waiting for outcomes excruciating: waiting for a project to get off the ground, news about a job promotion, or outcome of a health crisis.

As you wait, you don't have to drum your fingers. Try adopting a different attitude. What about learning to accept life on its own terms, allowing it to determine the pace of how things happen? Think about it. You usually have to wait for things that are worth waiting for. Remind yourself that it's worth waiting to get it right. When you realize life has its own rhythm, you don't expect the world to adapt to your speed. Once you slow down to fit into the natural harmony, it opens your heart and brings you a deep sense of serenity.

REVEL IN SOULFUL FEELINGS

Are you addicted to worldly feelings versus soul feelings? Here's what I mean. Contemplate the feelings

NOVEMBER

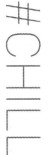

you get when someone applauds your work. Ponder what it feels like when you win a game, a bet, or an argument, when you succeed at something. Now contrast those feelings with a second set of emotions that arise when you watch a sunset, embrace a loved one, or become absorbed in a fulfilling task.

Contrast this set of soulful feelings with the first set of worldly feelings. Notice that feelings of self-glorification are empty of the nurturance and open-heartedness we feel when we enjoy the companionship of family, friends, or business associates. Observe yourself over the course of this month. Notice the actions you perform for the sake of attention, approval, or fame. Return to your openhearted feelings as often as you can.

COUNT YOUR BLESSINGS

When you overinvest in your job, you probably toil with an underlying belief that there's never enough. If you slack off, you'll lose your mojo and become a slacker. So you carry the distorted view of what needs doing, what's missing, or what didn't work. Maybe you even gripe about what you haven't achieved when your life is already abundant? During the week of Thanksgiving consider pausing from the ball games, parades, the turkey and stuffing and piles of work and contemplate all you're thankful for. You might discover that you're more fulfilled when you diminish your wants and give thanks for the blessings you already have.

No doubt you're thankful for your family, loved ones, and friends who have touched your life. And what about the new healthy thoughts and feelings you have developed, the food on the table, shelter over your head, and your health? You're fortunate to have 86,400 seconds today. Make them count by taking a few of them to meditate on everyone and everything for which you are thankful. Then go eat and watch the football game.

BE DRAWN, NOT DRIVEN

There is a big difference between being driven and being drawn. In the grip of work/life imbalance, you are driven by external circumstances. You relinquish your personal power to outside pressures. Driven by the ego, you allow them to determine your destiny.

Once in recovery from overworking, you discover an inner barometer to guide your thoughts. You move to an openhearted, soulful leadership—from being driven by deadlines to being drawn from a positive, personal calling from within.

Meditate on how much of your life is under the control of external factors versus internal sources.

NOVEMBER

#CHILL

Contemplate on how much of your life is driven instead of drawn from your heart and soul. Then ask yourself what actions you can take to change so you're led from a deeper, soulful source.

SEEK CONSCIOUS SPIRITUAL CONTACT

Step 11 of Workaholics Anonymous says, "We sought through prayer and meditation to improve our conscious contact with God as we understood God, praying only for knowledge of God's will for us and the power to carry that out."

Finding and living with conscious spiritual contact nurtures your inner needs. You devote yourself to prayer and meditation because it's the only direct experience you can have of knowing God and an inner life beyond your daily work and family. Along with conscious contact, you will notice that mental burdens, unnecessary worry, and wandering thoughts drop off one by one, and the void is replaced with peace and serenity and abundant moments to chill.

Perhaps you have moved away from your childhood religion and early understanding of God. Step 11 renews that search and often takes you on a different journey into Western and Eastern faiths and philosophies where you find loving communities to share your conscious spiritual contact. Your search helps you see the connections among all living beings and the importance of a daily spiritual practice, whether it's through meditation, prayer, self-introspection, the Golden Rule, world peace, or environmental harmony.

NOVEMBER TAKEAWAYS

- Take five minutes every day to practice chair yoga and conscious abdominal breathing.

- Recognize you are a package deal: equally your failures and your successes.

- Learn to wait without drumming your fingers or fidgeting in your seat.

- Sense the difference between worldly and soulful feelings each day.

- Give thanks to everyone who holds life steady while you conduct business.

- Meditate on being drawn from a spiritual place instead of being driven by demands.

- Improve conscious contact with your Higher Power through prayer and/or meditation.

- Be as willing to accept constructive criticism as much as you are praise.

DECEMBER

Your work is going to fill a large part of your life, and the only way to be truly satisfied is to do what you believe is great work.

—STEVE JOBS

GREAT WORK

The twelfth and final month of December signals the end of another year. The first full month of winter ushers in snowflakes in the Northern Hemisphere. And the monthly readings that thawed your heart over the past eleven months warms the chill in the air. Perhaps you cozy up to a fire or under a blanket with a good book and your favorite hot beverage to contemplate the meaning and significance of this month.

Multicultural celebrations of Hanukkah, Christmas, and Kwanzaa incorporate timeless rituals passed down for generations. The winter solstice marks the shortest day and the longest night of the year. And December marks Bodhi Day for Buddhists—the day the Buddha (which means Awakened One) sat under a tree until he rose enlightened. Perhaps the most important thread in all these ceremonies is giving to others: baking your favorite holiday treats, shopping for presents, and simple gifts of lovingkindness.

This month of gifting is a culmination of all the others, so it is only befitting that you consider the concept of "Great Work"—the act of selfless service and giving back what you have received. "Great Work" is both a congrats for practicing the mindfulness exercises from your reading as well as a commitment to pay forward the gifts you have received. You probably hear the compliment "great work" tossed around the office or sports field from time to time. You show your understanding of what "Great Work" really is—not by toiling sixty or seventy hours a week to gain top salesperson of the year, throwing all-nighters to reach a deadline, or juggling so many projects you have no time left for other life endeavors. You recognize that it also encompasses teamwork, passion, integrity, vision, ethics, and lovingkindness. It extends beyond mere job performance to staying mindfully engaged with yourself as a shining inspiration while sharing the knowledge you have attained from your own experience of chilling your life. Conscious, awake, and aware, you are intentional about being mindful and living in the present moment.

You give freely of yourself, not out of obligation, but out of compassion. Maybe you take a new employee under your wing or start a meditation group at your job. Great Work treats people of all walks of life—from janitor to judge—with the same respect, courtesy, and kind words. Perhaps you give a harried grocery shopper a spot in line, throw a kind smile to the equally harried checkout clerk, or wave forward a frustrated commuter trying to edge between you and the car in front.

In this chapter, you have a chance to practice your version of Great Work, bring your life into a fuller balance, and spread your message of mindful work/life integration in all your affairs. You can consider the simple but meaningful gifts of selfless service and what that might look like. Or you can ask what message you could carry to others from the changes you have made in your life without preaching, lecturing, or expecting anything in return. We are all basically the same human beings, mirrors of one another. What you keep to yourself you lose; what you give away you keep forever. When you do for others, you do for you. When you do Great Work for others, you do Great Work for yourself.

PRACTICE OPEN AWARENESS

When you take time out from your busy schedule to be still, you get to directly experience your mind and heart coexisting in the present moment. Take time out now to relate to your work in an open, wise, and enlivened way.

Eyes open, in your office or a private place, sit up straight on a chair or a floor cushion and open your awareness, paying attention to the vividness of the moment. Perhaps you notice the sounds of traffic off in

DECEMBER

the distance, a buzzing bee outside an opened window, or your own gurgling stomach. You might notice how shadows dance against the wall, a tree bending with the breeze, or the angle of sunlight beaming through a window. You might note the smell of something cooking or a flower's perfume, the feel of fabric, the taste of an apple wedge. Just stay mindful and open for a few more minutes.

If thoughts pop into your head about unfinished work or what you have to do next, gently bring your attention back to your breath and your open awareness. After you've immersed into the present moment for a period of time, transfer your attention to your mind and body. Notice how much calmer and more alert you feel inside.

DON'T POSTPONE JOY

When you think about how fleeting life is, what comes to mind that needs attention? If you had your life to live over, what would you do differently? One anonymous writer answered that question with, "If I had my life to live over, I'd have talked less and listened more. I'd have burned the candle sculpted like a rose before it melted in storage. I'd have gone to bed when I was sick instead of worrying that the Earth would go into a holding pattern if I missed work."

Think of three of your favorite things that bring you comfort or joy. Now ask yourself when the last time was that you did each one. What does this information tell you about how you're living your life? Are you living meaningfully? Or are you living someone else's script? Tomorrow has no guarantees, so go for the gusto!

TRANSFORM THROUGH GOOD GRIEF

The day of my father's funeral, I worked while my mother and sisters broke bread with neighbors. I was holed up in my university office twenty-five miles away working on a project so insignificant I no longer remember what it was. I didn't realize it then, but my work addiction numbed me to the grief.

By adulthood, most of us have lost someone we hold dear. A time will come when you must say goodbye to someone you love. Taking time out to grieve helps you feel and release the hurt and pain of the deep loss. If you're not in touch with your feelings, chances are the grief is so overwhelming you immerse yourself in work to avoid the pain. But that doesn't make it go away. If you don't take the time to mourn your losses, you will lack the time to mend. The more you store your emotions in the deep freeze, the more the frozen feelings will continue to paralyze you in ways you might not notice.

DECEMBER

Whatever you don't transform through grief, you transfer to others in one way or another. Have you put your grief on ice? If so, who or what do you need to say goodbye to? When and how will you mourn the loss so you can move forward with your life? When the time is right, meditate on each positive memory you have of the relationship and say silently, "I say goodbye to that memory." After releasing each memory, say, "I release myself from the past with you, ready to enter the present."

PRACTICE WALKING MEDITATION

I was fortunate enough to be led, along with a few hundred others, in a walking meditation by the Buddhist monk Thich Nhat Hanh. The experience was a memory I will always cherish. The good news is that you, too, can enjoy walking meditation. For many people, it is the equivalent of going to church. It allows you to let go of sorrows and worries—to get out of your mind and experience inner peace, gratitude, and compassion.

Here are some guidelines if you want to give it a shot. As you walk, place your attention fully on your feet and legs as you lift them and put them on the ground. Notice your feet making contact inside your shoes and then the ground. Pay attention to one foot and leg and the sensations as they carry you forward. Then shift to the other foot and leg. Drink in the sensations as they mobilize you. If you notice your mind drifting into other thoughts, let that be okay. Just bring your awareness back to the sensations of your feet as they connect to the ground. Walk as if you're kissing the earth with your feet. With each step, allow yourself to be filled with freedom from your mind's burdens.

STOP LABELING YOURSELF

The ways in which you think about change can make a difference. Labels are for jars and frozen foods, not humans. They keep you stuck in whatever bad habit you're trying to break. You're not a worrywart, control freak, sad sack, or penny pincher. Perhaps you're trying to worry less, let go of control, think happier thoughts, or save money.

When you use active instead of static language, you're on the path to your Higher Self with a capital *S*. Ask yourself if you use labels to describe yourself or others. Notice how the label boxes in people and stunts their growth. Ask what action words you can apply, then pay attention to how much better that feels inside and how much easier it is to chill.

COME HOME

Where are you most weeknights at 7 P.M.? Still working? You can get so caught up in your job that you don't stop to think that somebody needs you at home: a spouse, child, pet, or perhaps a parent.

Truth be told, it's a wonderful gift when a person loves you enough to wonder where you are and wants to be with you. How fortunate you are to have someone waiting for you—someone who anticipates seeing you—when many people spend lonely nights of quiet desperation. Stop and ask who waits for you to come home. Do you appreciate their anticipation? Or does it feel like a burden? Do you ignore or reject them on a regular basis? Or do you let their love for you melt your heart?

BE A TEAM PLAYER

Is it hard for you to work as a team? And do you operate best alone? If you rule with an iron fist, you are probably motivated by fear and loss of status. Reluctant to take chances to achieve creative outcomes, perhaps you try to avoid mistakes or cover them up. If so, that prevents you from being a good collaborator, delegator, or team player. You believe your approach and style are the best answers and have difficulty entertaining "less perfect ideas."

Teamwork is essential for success in the workplace. Creative solutions to diverse problems come from a team approach that can generate many possibilities. And learning to be a team member is essential for recovery from compulsive overworking. The Rx is for you to release your need to be in charge and learn to collaborate. You can become a creative risk taker willing to stretch beyond customary bounds and a master of self-correction who learns from your mistakes.

Contemplate how you perform as a collaborator, delegator, or team player in your job. Are you good at teamwork, self-correction, and creative risk taking? Can you use your skills in a different way than you're currently using them?

SEEK STILLNESS

You are immersed in a twenty-first-century culture that mistakes loudness for authority, yelling for substance. Once your feet hit the floor, you race against the clock shaking your fist at the heavens. The chaos of your tasks defines you. In these ways, you unwittingly create your own stress and worry.

When you have at least as much interest in what happens inside as on the outside, it brings quiet to the noise of daily living. Once you make an appointment with yourself to simply be, you shift your focus from

#CHILL

doing to being and your life changes for the better. You connect with that place of stillness that dwells deep within you, a sanctuary where you can retreat from the hectic world to gain renewal.

When was the last time you felt the stillness around and inside you? No horns blowing, no screaming voices, no loud music, lawn mowers, or weed eaters. Not even the screams of your inner critic telling you to get busy. Just the stillness of your breath, the peacefulness of a tree limb covered with softly fallen snow, or a spiderweb sprinkled with early morning dew of gold and scarlet from the sun's reflection. Are you willing to allow these scenes to teach you stillness?

ILLUMINATE YOUR BLIND SPOTS

Sometimes—perhaps much of the time—you have blind spots. You see the world, the workplace, and friends and family as you are—not as they are. Blind to the needs and perspectives of others, you stay focused straight ahead, setting your sights on projects, problem solving, and troubleshooting. As you rush forward with your work blinders, you miss many of life's important moments along the way: birthdays, anniversaries, holidays, and family reunions.

You owe it to yourself and to the ones you love and work with to remain fully aware in your daily life, mindful of taking moments to chill, weighing your options and the consequences before allowing work commitments to engulf your life.

Meditate on where your blind spots are. What or who have you overlooked? What blinders do you need to remove to bring your life into greater perspective and fuller work/life integration?

TAKE OFF THE MASK

If you're like most driven workers, you pretend you're a powerful decision maker, that you have all the answers, that you're unruffled by hurtful things people say, that you're calm in the face of turmoil, and that you don't need anyone else in your life. Deep inside, you know this is not true at all. You know the truth and are aware that it's only a mask you wear to get through the day.

After years of hurt, you push your feelings deeper inside. You wear a mask to prevent others from seeing who you really are and to avoid your own feelings. You plunge deeper into work, losing touch with yourself altogether.

If you want to chill from frantic overdoing, you will have to look behind the mask and ask yourself what feelings smolder underneath. What is denied? What is unfelt? What needs to be reached before you explode?

DECEMBER

As you face your feelings with honesty, you come to understand yourself in a way that you never have before. You grow and start to feel fully human.

Contemplate your impenetrable mask and what it would take to stop hiding from yourself or pretending to be someone you're not. Ask yourself what would happen if you removed the mask once and for all and lived today as you truly are.

INTUIT

When you overrely on your logical mind, it can eclipse intuition or a knowing deep in your heart. Intuition is the soft inner voice that speaks to you when you get still and quiet.

As you seek to integrate your work and personal life, you can mix logic and intuition in order to create more balance. In combination, they help you make important decisions. When you can go to a quiet place in your heart and ask for guidance, your intuition guides you to the next right job, the best way to handle conflict, or a loving way to treat yourself.

Find a quiet place where you can be still and turn within. Contemplate an issue you've struggled with. It could be ways to improve a relationship with a coworker or decisions about the direction of your career. With eyes closed, ask the question, listen, and be mindful of any answers that might come to you. Don't give up if it doesn't come right away. Be patient until you get an answer.

MAKE A TO-BE LIST

Are you as notorious as many frenzied work junkies are for making a list of all the things that you need to do? Do you draw them up, check them twice, and make sure every item is checked off before you end the day? List making often evolves into overscheduling and overcommitting so that you're constantly racing against the clock.

But what if you made a to-be list alongside your to-do list? What would you put on it? I make it a practice to have a to-be list. One item always on my list is to be outdoors in nature and listen to the natural sounds on a regular basis: birds tweeting, insects in the bushes, or frogs croaking. If you were to start your list now, you might list elbow room to stretch and breathe between appointments or fifteen minutes to an hour each day to relax, exercise, play, meditate, pray, practice deep breathing, or just contemplate the universe.

Meditate on some items you might put on your to-be list. Jot down a few of the items. As you complete them, check them off in the next few days. If you

DECEMBER

have to add a new task to your to-do list, knock another one off and make sure your to-be list is equal in length so you don't get overloaded.

TRY NOVELTY

Your daily routines can be a double-edged sword. They make life easier and more comfortable in some ways, and they add an element of predictability and organization. But they can make it harder to embrace new experiences, which are powerful sources of resilience and happiness. Seeking sameness and avoiding challenges leads to boredom and limits your full potential.

Test-drive some ways you can bring novelty into your work or personal life. Try new things. Meet different colleagues for lunch, develop a new skill, or take a different route to the workplace. Dare to think bigger every day and you'll grow to new heights.

CELEBRATE THE REAL HOLIDAYS

The term "wedded to work" was coined for a good reason, and it knows no gender boundaries. More people put more time and energy into work than into family relationships, socializing with friends, hobbies, or leisure and recreational activities. Studies show that nightly family dinnertime has become a dinosaur of yore with 70 percent of meals consumed outside the home and 20 percent eaten in the car. Holidays are just another day to get work done from dawn to dusk. While others celebrate Hanukkah, Christmas, or Kwanzaa, chances are you forget, ignore, or minimize holidays, birthdays, reunions, or anniversaries.

Holidays and family celebrations are the glue that creates family cohesion. When you don't uphold the rituals, over time family relationships tend to unravel. It's important to remind yourself to come up for air during holidays. You have a choice to participate in the festivities and religious aspects of your holidays by enjoying the music, cooking special foods, or having get-togethers without getting caught up in the "holidaze." You don't have to overdo it or let the materialism and commercialization overwhelm you. You can decide how you want to celebrate and what true meaning and enjoyment you get from this time of year.

DEVELOP GOOD HABITS

You might be loath to admit that you have habits that aid and abet work addiction—bad habits that you would like to break or good habits that you would like to cultivate so you can chill more often. There was a time when my endless promises to stop

DECEMBER

smoking, eat better, and start exercising became distant memories.

Until I discovered the "If-then" strategy that helped me stick to the action part of my goals. My vague plan to exercise went from "I will exercise more" to "If x happens, then I'll do y." The x is the situation, and y is the action to take when x occurs. Plugging my idle vow to exercise into a specific action plan looked like this: "Every Tuesday and Thursday mornings at 8:00 A.M., I will meet my personal trainer at the gym for a one-hour workout." This strategy got me moving, and I've been at it for many years now.

So why does it work? The "If-then" strategy automatically hardwires your brain with a heightened vigilance to be on the lookout for a specific situation ("If I see fried foods on a restaurant menu") and the action that must follow ("then I will avoid them"). Experts say it takes about one month to break an old habit and replace it with a good one. Try setting a target goal to change one of your stressful habits by plugging your goal into the "If-then" formula: If x happens (the event), then I'll do y (action).

SCRUB OVERTHINKING

If you're an overthinker, you probably stay in your head a lot—overthinking too much of the time. Maybe you second-guess a job decision, rehearse an up-coming meeting, brood over a coworker's comment, or rehash a conversation in your head, stewing over a comment you made: "That was a dumb thing to say in yesterday's office meeting. Everyone must think I'm a jerk."

When you overthink your actions, it's like leaving your internal alarm system on 24/7. It's exhausting and stressful, creates anxiety and depression, and hampers your interactions with coworkers and loved ones. Chronic overthinkers dwell on the past and con-jure up catastrophic images of the future. Instead of solving problems, overthinkers amplify small things and stay stuck in their heads. This leads to emotional paralysis and inaction and adds to misery.

If you catch yourself ruminating about a work or family problem, train yourself to move from focusing on the problem into brainstorming possible solutions. Change your perspective from overthinking's restricted thoughts and pull up the big picture, which puts thoughts into a more balanced perspective. Always remind your-self that your manufactured thoughts are *your* thoughts and yours alone. Most people don't have the same perspective about you that you project onto them.

DECEMBER

GROUND YOURSELF

When you're busy around the clock, you spend a lot of time unaware of what's happening in your body. The practice of grounding puts you in touch with body sensations and broadens your awareness of the present moment. Grounding activates your rest-and-digest response and calms you down when you're undergoing stress.

Find a comfortable sitting position in a chair with a back to it. Sitting up straight, notice how the back of the chair is supporting your back. Bring your full attention to that area of support and focus there for one minute. Then bring your attention to your feet resting on the floor. Pay attention to the bottom of your feet and the support of the ground or floor underneath. Focus on that area of support for one minute. Next bring your attention to your bottom on the chair. Notice the support of the chair underneath your bottom and focus on that area for one minute.

After you ground, take another minute to notice the sensations of your breathing, heart rate, and muscle tone. Many people say they feel more relaxed, more in their bodies, and that breathing and heart rate slow down and muscle tone loosens. Now take one more minute to do a body scan from head to toe, being mindful of places inside that have changed in a positive way. Then bring your awareness back into your present space and notice how much more chilled you are.

FINISH UNFINISHED BUSINESS

It's a fact of life. If you haven't already, someday you will be brought to your knees. A diagnosis you didn't expect, a phone call you never imagined, or a loss you cannot endure will bring an ending. Endings offer you a breakdown and a breakthrough—an opportunity for deeper growth and fulfillment as you move forward. As you honor the endings in your life and acknowledge their impact on you, they fill you with grief.

Out of your grief you discover that you're ending and beginning all at the same time—that from an ending something is born. New Year's Eve ushers in a new year. The end of summer must begin the fall. To end something is to start something. The end is where you begin.

Moving forward, ask yourself what loose ends in your work and personal life need tying up. After you end the unfinished, fresh starts are born. What long-held emotions need resolution? What projects need completion? What relationships need attention? And what needs to happen so that your endings bring you healthy beginnings anew?

DECEMBER

GIVE BACK

Step 12 of Workaholics Anonymous says, "Having had a spiritual awakening as the result of these steps, we tried to carry this message to workaholics and to practice these principles in all our affairs."

This Step is a culmination of the others as you return to the world what you received. You give freely of yourself, not out of obligation, but out of love. Perhaps you get involved with an employee assistance program at work, start a discussion group to prevent burnout on the job, take a new employee under your wing, become someone's Twelve Step sponsor, or simply practice the principles and shine as an inspiration.

What you keep to yourself you lose; what you give away you keep forever. Putting the Twelve Steps into practice helps you connect from the heart after working from your head most of your life. Relationships become healthier, and positive people come into your life. Your deeds and actions attract others who are also seeking ways to chill with a healthy work/life balance. You share your message of work addiction and spiritual growth without preaching, lecturing, or advising and without expecting anything in return. As a result of your spiritual awakening, the cycle perpetuates itself. You are spiritually strengthened by the messages and transformation of others which, in turn, enrich your own life a thousand fold.

DECEMBER TAKEAWAYS

- Celebrate festive occasions—and regular ones—with loved ones for more meaningful moments.
- Commit to removing your blinders, observing your blind spots, and seeing your world more clearly.
- Ground yourself throughout the day in body awareness so you can stay in the present moment.
- Remember to carry the message of mindful work/life integration to others, learn to chill, and give back in all your affairs.
- Finish unfinished business and start anew with dedicated mindfulness practices, living in present-moment awareness.
- Find your inner sanctuary where you can retreat, be still, and chill anytime.
- Get out of your head, tune out your job, and tune in to your life.

DECEMBER

366
CHILLERS

January 1   I take time to inventory my life, and I put temporary scaffolding in place.

January 2   I monitor the overpowering urge to overload myself.

January 3   I practice moment-to-moment reflection of my inner life and my environment.

January 4 I practice self-care.

January 5 I admit that I have flaws and embrace each one.

January 6 I practice being fully present with loved ones and coworkers.

January 7 I ask myself if I'm jumping to conclusions before I take negative predictions as fact.

January 8 I welcome idle moments as gifts.

January 9 I take back the power I turned over to my work.

January 10 I overcome workplace obstacles by pinpointing the opportunities hidden in difficulties.

January 11 I take responsibility for my thoughts, feelings, and actions.

January 12 I realize that when life offers many possible outcomes, I become calm and focused on the tasks at hand.

January 13 I practice patience and comfort while waiting for important decisions to incubate.

January 14   I break the habit of scheduling myself too tightly.

January 15   I express myself in ways that are natural to me.

January 16   I strive to see the gains in my losses and the beginnings in my endings.

January 17   I don't allow my work to overwhelm me.

January 18   I pay close attention to how I treat my loved ones.

January 19   I take a hard look at my life and start to make healthy changes.

January 20   I muster the courage to endure the sharp pains of self-discovery.

January 21   I appreciate my life and seize the day so that tomorrow brings no regrets.

January 22   I take time out to sit with my troubles with nonjudgmental lovingkindness.

January 23   I recognize there's nothing else to do but the next right thing.

366 CHILLERS

January 24 I reflect on how I can improve my attitude.

January 25 I experience first zingers without having second-zinger reactions.

January 26 I know where to draw the line and view this as a gift to myself and others.

January 27 I continue to climb through tough times.

January 28 Today I am. Yesterday I was. Tomorrow I will be.

January 29 I welcome my emotions with openheartedness to others.

January 30 I pinpoint what my criticisms of others mirror about me.

January 31 I accept life on its own terms.

February 1 I pay compassionate, nonjudgmental attention to what I'm thinking and feeling.

February 2 I pay attention to the energy I bring to face the workday.

February 3   I remember the acronym HALT and take necessary action to chill.

February 4   I ask for clarity to save myself unnecessary worry and stress.

February 5   I recognize when overworking bars me from opening my heart to others and myself.

February 6   I give myself permission to concentrate on the truly important things.

February 7   I practice mindful eating and drinking.

February 8   I practice intentional gratitude. I want what I have instead of wanting what I don't have.

February 9   I cultivate how I want to think and feel.

February 10   I welcome self-approval as I build my resources to face everyday challenges.

February 11   I want the best for myself and affirm my efforts as I would a best friend or a colleague.

February 12   I take myself off red alert when I am home and pace myself during the workday.

366 CHILLERS

#CHILL

February 13   I create paths that lead to my hopes and dreams.

February 14   I offer my love language to the important people in my life and send love in their languages.

February 15   I understand that my work sustainability over the long haul depends on how balanced my life is now.

February 16   I listen to my body when it talks to me.

February 17   I choose my self-talk carefully to comfort, support, and build courage.

February 18   I love myself unconditionally.

February 19   I release the negative thoughts that stream through my mind.

February 20   I view my own voice as my final stamp of approval.

February 21   I strive toward living a life that I am happy with.

February 22   I look beyond what I do or accomplish to affirm my worth.

February 23   I practice honesty and trustworthiness in all my affairs.

February 24   I cultivate more passionate approaches to connect with my soul.

February 25   I remind myself of the blessings that disguise themselves in hardship.

February 26   I ask not how is life treating me, but how I am treating life.

February 27   I unplug from electronic devices to enjoy life's other pleasures.

February 28   I express gratitude for all the fullness that I already have.

February 29   I choose to soar in my spiritual search.

March 1   I vow to take care of my body.

March 2   I broaden my vantage point to see the world as it really is.

366 CHILLERS

March 3   I integrate a good night's sleep into my regimen.

March 4   I release compulsive thoughts that create imbalanced thinking.

March 5   I vow to treat my mind, body, and spirit with compassion and respect.

March 6   I give myself the gift of flexibility.

March 7   I use hardships to become more resilient.

March 8   I don't fear falling down.

March 9   I appreciate the richness of the present moment as it connects me to myself and the deep richness of my life.

March 10   I listen for times when my stinkin' thinkin' creates blind spots.

March 11   I choose to use my time calmly and compassionately.

March 12   I distance myself from criticism.

March 13   I show compassion to further enrich my own life.

March 14 I set goals in each sphere of my life.

March 15 I free myself from materialism and accolades.

March 16 I vow to spend more time on things that are important, not just urgent.

March 17 I give up the need to impose my will on life's conditions.

March 18 I treat myself like I would a best friend.

March 19 I give up the fears of not being good enough and of losing control of my life.

March 20 I am an active participant with others who depend on me.

March 21 I let Mother Nature transport me out of the artificial world of electronics and fast-paced deadlines.

March 22 I give myself the gift of being present in each moment.

March 23 I talk to myself in endearing terms.

March 24 I remember I have access to positivity anytime.

366 CHILLERS

March 25   I ask if I'm treating my loved ones with the integrity and respect they deserve.

March 26   I open myself to the possibility of editing or rewriting my narrative.

March 27   I unplug after work to become a better worker, spouse, and parent.

March 28   I free myself from mind traps.

March 29   I view love as who I am and who I'm becoming.

March 30   I see myself on a healing path.

March 31   I use clarity and self-insight to view my worries and frustrations as relics of the past.

April 1   I practice mindful connection with my breath to be more centered and productive.

April 2   I set clearer, more reachable work goals.

April 3   I resist nothing.

April 4   I take some time off from work activities to do things that bring me joy or satisfaction.

April 5   I provide an incubation period for my work ambitions.

April 6   I refrain from believing or identifying with negative thoughts.

April 7   I face conflict with an open, compassionate mind.

April 8   I don't let my internal dialogue distract me from the present moment.

April 9   I choose just one thing to do that I've done before and do it differently.

April 10   I find beauty in the ordinary.

April 11   I let go of my negative reactions when things don't go my way.

April 12   I face worry, criticism, and fear with courage.

April 13   I forgive myself.

April 14   I thaw any frozen emotions.

April 15   I surrender to whatever happens.

366 CHILLERS

April 16 I focus on worry as a separate part of me.

April 17 I view each experience as an opportunity to grow in resilience, love, and kindness.

April 18 I strive to work in a more humane way.

April 19 I take a renewed interest in the lives of loved ones.

April 20 I decide what's critical for my work effectiveness and what's blocking it.

April 21 I bring as much intention to my personal life as I bring to my work life.

April 22 I ask what I can do to be kinder to the planet on which I live.

April 23 I toss my old grudges away.

April 24 I improve working relationships with colleagues.

April 25 I am spontaneous, flexible, and collaborative.

April 26 I live with uncertainty.

April 27 I stretch through my fears of intimacy and strive for acceptance.

April 28 I harness strength from places where I feel broken.

April 29 I celebrate mealtimes.

April 30 I take stock in the traits that fuel my work addiction without devaluing myself.

May 1 I chant to clear my mind of stressful work thoughts and my body of tense muscles.

May 2 I put more time into self-reflection.

May 3 I prioritize exercise.

May 4 I don't let job stress metastasize into my personal time.

May 5 I take time to soften my heart and connect with myself.

May 6 I pace myself throughout the workday.

May 7 I accept the multifaceted parts of myself.

366 CHILLERS

May 8   I welcome eustress that motivates me.

May 9   I grow comfortable with serenity.

May 10   I begin each day with inner fortitude.

May 11   I resolve to live a healthier and more balanced life.

May 12   I check out the facts before drawing conclusions to save myself unnecessary worry.

May 13   I excavate my True Self, which has been covered up by life's demands.

May 14   I take leadership of my life.

May 15   I manage my devices instead of letting them manage me.

May 16   I take time off from work to restore my mind and body.

May 17   I stay grounded after negative episodes at work.

May 18   I reframe negative thoughts by looking at them from more than one standpoint.

May 19 I am aware of my mental reactions to stress without giving in.

May 20 I choose activities I enjoy.

May 21 I observe stressful emotional states until the discomfort subsides.

May 22 I share my problems with people I love.

May 23 I slow down my work life.

May 24 I refuse to sell myself short at work or in relationships.

May 25 I put work in one quadrant of my life and fill the other three with play, self-care, and intimate relationships.

May 26 I call upon my curiosity as the gateway to clarity.

May 27 I sometimes put self-care before work commitments.

May 28 I will never give up.

366 CHILLERS

May 29   I am not enslaved by my work schedule.

May 30   I look through fresh, mindful eyes.

May 31   I eliminate self-deception.

June 1   I pay closer attention to my workday and become mindful of my surroundings.

June 2   I look for the positive side of a negative situation.

June 3   I rejoice in others' good fortune.

June 4   I see my shortcomings for what they are.

June 5   I take positive action to unlock a range of possibilities.

June 6   I recognize that clear-mindedness reduces black-and-white thinking.

June 7   I unearth greater courage within myself.

June 8   I look for humans who support my recovery from work addiction.

June 9   I find ways to relax.

June 10 I send imposter syndrome packing.

June 11 I soothe the anxious part of me.

June 12 I ditch rigid expectations.

June 13 I see that my life is unfolding exactly as it's supposed to.

June 14 I recognize that important changes take time.

June 15 I give my mind a rest from imperatives.

June 16 I approach life with forethought.

June 17 I invite good humor into the workplace.

June 18 I communicate my needs honestly and directly.

June 19 I create shock absorbers for my busy schedule.

June 20 I realize I don't have to be superhuman at work.

June 21 I look for spiritual footing that renews my sense of meaning and purpose.

366 CHILLERS

#CHILL

June 22 I learn to act and roll with the punches.

June 23 I am efficient at work without sacrificing reasonable hours.

June 24 I take time to give myself a pep talk.

June 25 I tell myself I can withstand just about any curveball life throws at me.

June 26 I make the distinction between loneliness and solitude.

June 27 I calm myself by challenging perceived threats.

June 28 I conduct my personal and business affairs without being combative.

June 29 I remind myself that I am more powerful than my procrastination.

June 30 I permit myself to be the real deal.

July 1 I practice doing nothing for several minutes each day.

July 2 I distinguish between essential and nonessential tasks.

July 3 I reject "if onlies" and "only ifs."

July 4 I do not let life's curveballs dictate my well-being at work or home.

July 5 I celebrate National Workaholics Day by doing anything other than facing paperwork and the computer.

July 6 I welcome the present moment.

July 7 I practice taking the perception of "the beginner's mind."

July 8 I curb cravings for high drama at work.

July 9 I let creativity come to fruition on its own.

July 10 I observe unpleasant self-talk in my head with curiosity instead of judgment.

July 11 I am strong and self-reliant.

July 12 I measure my worth by my ability to display my True Self.

July 13 I let enthusiasm carry me through the workday.

366 CHILLERS

CHILL

July 14   I bring my compulsive overworking into balance.

July 15   I remember that the power inside me is greater than the obstacles before me.

July 16   I give tender, loving self-care to myself.

July 17   I make work a star instead of the sun.

July 18   I am in charge of my mind, not the other way around.

July 19   I don't cling to perfection.

July 20   I realize a positive outlook empowers me with greater confidence.

July 21   I have nothing to fear or hide anymore.

July 22   I infuse natural life into my workday.

July 23   I perform good deeds without expecting to receive something back.

July 24   I accept job uncertainty because it's beyond my control.

July 25 I summon inner strength to cope with the challenges of workaholism recovery.

July 26 I develop greater faith in my abilities.

July 27 I slow down and bend myself to life's schedule.

July 28 I recharge my batteries by creating a work-free zone.

July 29 I go on with my life instead of postponing it.

July 30 I take risks and make mistakes.

July 31 I am ready to have my shortcomings removed.

August 1 I strive to live life in the present.

August 2 I lighten my workdays with less doing and more being.

August 3 I am ever mindful that my words can harm or heal.

August 4 I trust that doors of opportunity will open for me.

366 CHILLERS

 # CHILL

August 5   I remind myself where abundance exists in my life.

August 6   I overcome emotional pain from the past.

August 7   I look inside my heart for the answers that I'm used to searching for in my head.

August 8   I break out of rigidity by bending with the curves.

August 9   I ask what my hands have done lately to take better care of me.

August 10   I let go of the lesser things to make room for the greater good.

August 11   I use each setback as a lesson to build my fortitude.

August 12   I brainstorm better solutions.

August 13   I grow from whatever comes my way.

August 14   I ask myself what edge my inhibitions can give me.

August 15   I do my best.

August 16   I affirm my accomplishments.

August 17   I remember there's more happening around and inside me than I realize.

August 18   I explore the gray areas.

August 19   I find happiness on the inside first.

August 20   I design the life I want.

August 21   I work with compassion and consideration for the ones I serve.

August 22   I live in the present.

August 23   I reframe my outlook.

August 24   I get up just one more time than I fall.

August 25   I let the yearning of my heart teach me about alignment with others and self-fulfillment.

August 26   I prioritize my connections with others.

366 CHILLERS

August 27   I view my life as worth celebrating.

August 28   I set boundaries at work so I have time to play.

August 29   I spend time intentionally honoring my Higher Self.

August 30   I realize I have all the time I need to do what needs completion.

August 31   I make amends to everyone I harmed through my overworking.

September 1   I bow to moments of awe in my life.

September 2   I create special moments with loved ones.

September 3   I make simple changes to my workspace so that it's more visually appealing.

September 4   I examine the work habits that upset my balance.

September 5   I recognize I don't always know what motivates the actions of others.

September 6   I try to come face-to-face with the roots of my compulsive overworking.

September 7 I refrain from taking the naysayer voice in my head too seriously.

September 8 I have everything I need to succeed within my reach.

September 9 I don't have to finish everything right away.

September 10 I realize that I am not always in control of the outcomes.

September 11 I give myself pep talks when I am riddled with self-doubt.

September 12 I think before I leap.

September 13 I practice smiling until it becomes natural.

September 14 I pay curious attention to my stress.

September 15 I live each day as though it were my last.

September 16 I remind myself that everything isn't an emergency.

September 17 I revisit the Twelve-Step program of Workaholics Anonymous to kick compulsive work habits.

366 CHILLERS

September 18   I laugh more.

September 19   I practice the Ten Commandments of Self-Care.

September 20   I refrain from overscheduling.

September 21   I commit to stop feeding old resentments.

September 22   I discover how to unconditionally love myself.

September 23   I value a rich internal life.

September 24   I commit to active family participation.

September 25   I know there's a limit to how much I can expect.

September 26   I set the tone of my workday by creating personal daily goals that coexist with company goals.

September 27   My ecstasy comes from connection to my compassionate, healthy, and spiritual Self.

September 28   My creative instincts come from a different place inside than my compulsive overworking.

September 29   I replace exaggerated words like *always* and *never* with balanced words such as *sometimes* and *often*.

September 30   I change bad behaviors into more considerate and caring ones.

October 1   I devote to going inward on a regular basis.

October 2   I think and feel more kindly.

October 3   I don't focus on being right.

October 4   I acknowledge all the people who sacrificed their time to help me.

October 5   I convey my perspective with gentle assertiveness.

October 6   I am mindful of today.

October 7   I rewire workaholic tendencies.

366 CHILLERS

October 8   I don't jump to assigning meaning to events.

October 9   I cultivate healthy work habits that can boost my success.

October 10   I make room for daily unexpected situations.

October 11   I meditate on creating a new normal.

October 12   I practice turnarounds instead of waiting for the experience to change.

October 13   I wrap myself in the priorities.

October 14   I embrace the small catastrophes and big challenges.

October 15   I don't wonder how and when life will happen to me.

October 16   I go outside more.

October 17   I practice Great Work.

October 18   I keep it simple.

October 19 I note my defensive behaviors.

October 20 I realize that a piece of me also lives in every person I encounter.

October 21 I look for hard evidence before assuming the worst.

October 22 I say yes more.

October 23 I use work in a healthy way to create a fulfilling life.

October 24 I bring healthy balance to my life.

October 25 I let myself shine.

October 26 I reconsider my attitude.

October 27 I start to make conscious choices moment to moment.

October 28 I make it a point to do as many of my bucket-list items as I can.

October 29 I recognize how far I've come.

October 30 I look for reasons to open my heart.

366 CHILLERS

#CHILL

October 31 I take stock of my mistakes and let go of them.

November 1 I practice yoga in my office chair.

November 2 I silence the critical voices in my own head.

November 3 I pay attention to my tendency to avoid unpleasant people and situations.

November 4 I trust feedback from people I trust.

November 5 I never quit trying.

November 6 I practice Right View in my personal and professional life.

November 7 I practice conscious abdominal breathing.

November 8 I reignite relationships with others.

November 9 I pause to understand my internal landscape.

November 10 I mine my inner resources.

November 11 I stay at a distance from upsetting events.

November 12 I think of the inherent value I bring to the job.

November 13 I find hobbies that bring me more energy.

November 14 I'm learning to live from the *inside out* instead of the *outside in*.

November 15 I contemplate the pain that shows up in my life.

November 16 I use positive affirmations.

November 17 I am excited for my future successes.

November 18 I put my ego aside, and let my heart lead.

November 19 I realize life doesn't bend to fit my specifications.

November 20 I take myself off constant red alert.

November 21 I see how my loved ones bring so much value to our bond.

November 22 I don't make myself the victim.

366 CHILLERS

November 23   I let go of my addictive thoughts.

November 24   I try to reconnect with my soul.

November 25   I take time out to say thank you to those who really matter.

November 26   I pray for the courage to release grudges one by one.

November 27   I am fully committed to renounce being driven by work pressures.

November 28   I start to practice self-parenting my inner child.

November 29   I'm learning to let go of false beliefs.

November 30   I seek through meditation to improve my experience of life beyond work.

December 1   I cultivate practices that help me relate to work in a more open, wise, and enlivened way.

December 2   I live my life as much in the present as possible.

December 3   I fully experience the grief so it can soothe and heal me.

December 4   I always have a choice to experience bliss.

December 5   I consider a walking meditation to keep me centered.

December 6   I am mindful of not putting labels on other people or myself.

December 7   I seek a life purpose that provides fulfillment.

December 8   I pay more focused attention to loved ones.

December 9   I use my discontent to search deeper within myself for fulfillment.

December 10   I open myself to the creative flow of my colleagues.

December 11   I no longer allow my work schedule to enslave me.

December 12   I do less.

December 13   I let my surroundings ground me.

December 14   I pinpoint my blind spots.

366 CHILLERS

December 15   I trust that everything will be revealed to me in its own time.

December 16   I take one stone down from the wall I've built.

December 17   I strive not to be arrogant or cocky.

December 18   I do not overrely on my logical mind.

December 19   I complete my to-be list just as earnestly as I complete my to-do list.

December 20   I take pride in a life of integrity and mindful presence.

December 21   I am inspired by people I cross paths with on a regular basis.

December 22   I refrain from adding insult to injury.

December 23   I make a commitment to spicing things up.

December 24   I move through each day with compassion.

December 25 I celebrate the holidays in ways that are meaningful to my loved ones.

December 26 I make plans about when and where I will act on my goals.

December 27 I experience more happiness and joy.

December 28 I catch myself overanalyzing a problem and let it go.

December 29 I feel prepared for the routines of the day.

December 30 I heal my toxic attitudes and finish unfinished business.

December 31 I give freely and unselfishly.

366 CHILLERS

PARTING COMMENTS

Five Minutes a Day in Your Sweet Spot

Life is full of possibilities. Now that you have progressed through the twelve months of *#Chill*, you have everything you need to bring the possibilities into fruition and your life into balance. But just when the time comes that you think you've nailed it—that will be the beginning all over again. The poet T. S. Eliot said it best: "What we call the beginning is often the end. And to make an end is to make a beginning. The end is where we start from."

Achieving balance between *doing* (your job) and *being* (your personal life) is a never-ending dance. Especially in a culture where doing is more valued than being, and the adage "An idle mind is the devil's workshop" blinks in your brain like a neon sign. And you're taught to believe that the more you do the greater your worth. If you're like most people, you will continue to struggle to find that sweet spot—the middle way between doing and being. Life's curve balls will continue to track you down and challenge you on a daily basis. Some people (including yourself) will expect a lot from you and make unreasonable demands. Life won't go the way you want whether Mercury is in retrograde or not. And job pressures and family obligations will breathe down your neck. It might even feel like the world is conspiring against you at times. But it isn't.

Here's the good news. When you use the tools to chill from the inside out, calm and fulfillment will love you back from the outside in. Every time you get caught in the stress of the moment and take five minutes to step back and find opportunity in the difficulty, you get stronger, calmer, and happier. May you find that sweet spot where your busy life coexists with idle moments to chill—moments without imperatives, nothing to rush to, fix, or accomplish. The sweetness of doing nothing for the sheer pleasure of it. Just five minutes of "sweet nothings" where peace and serenity reside within. And you whisper to yourself the gift of being mindfully present in each moment.

Welcome home to the end where you start from and your new beginning. Keep chipping away at the frozen sea inside until a fully formed you is revealed, winking its clear, chill eye.

ACKNOWLEDGMENTS

This book began like a huge lump of clay, waiting to be molded and shaped into the final product you're holding in your hands. It took many people to help me chisel the words into a coherent, visually pleasing, and hopefully enjoyable and useful format. I don't believe in witchcraft, witch's brew, voodoo, or black magic, but I do believe in magic—the magic at the hands of talented and dedicated people whose support cast a spell all over this book to make it a reality.

First and foremost to my spouse, Jamey McCullers, (cousin of the legendary writer Carson McCullers): without your unwavering support, this book wouldn't exist. You didn't inherit Carson's writing gene, but you are a wizard at invoking an exotic backdrop of life and beauty, free of chaos and, throughout my writing career, speaking to me with a love language of "acts of service"—cooking meals, preventing interruptions from our three dogs, placing exotic orchids

ACKNOWLEDGMENTS

from your greenhouse on my writing desk, brewing a pot of potpourri to fill the house with alluring aromas, bringing me nutritious food and drinks, and generally keeping the ship afloat. You are my love potion, and I love you.

My deepest appreciation to my tireless agent, Dean Krystek, of Wordlink Literary Agency, for his steadfast belief in this project from the get-go and his perseverance in finding this book a home. I owe a debt of gratitude to JKS Communications and my publicists Sara Wigal and Max Lopez, who saw this project through from beginning to end with creative advice and support and to Abby Felder for suggesting I put # in front of Chill as the title of this book.

A huge shout-out to my editor, John Paine, who smoothed my words, making it easier and clearer for the reader. And to all my colleagues and friends at International Thriller Writers, who do the best job of any organization I know of supporting aspiring scribes, debut authors, and seasoned writers: Kimberley Howe, Jenny Milchman, Lee Child, Nancy Bilyeau, Dawn Ius, Steve Berry, M. J. Rose, Wendy Tyson, Barry Lancet, Elena Hartwell, and Sheila Sobel.

I want to thank my technical advisor, Charlie Covington, for his masterful help with formatting the manuscript and guidance on Internet and electronic issues. A huge shout-out to photo artist Jon Michael Riley for your generous time and creative genius with the photograph of Hudson and me on the book. And I am deeply appreciative of the wonderful team at HarperCollins/William Morrow. Thanks for believing in me. You were a joy to work with: Lisa Sharkey, senior vice president; Anna Montague, my editor; and Julie Paulauski, my publicist there. Your excitement and ingenuity were contagious and added so much to the final product.

I extend my appreciation to all the talented writers of diverse genres who took their valuable time to read the manuscript and write a blurb when they could have been penning their own work: Alanis Morissette, Harville Hendrix, Tara Brach, Amit Ray, Professor Mark Leary, and Professor Peg O'Conner. To my dear friends and family, who nurture and support me through the daily challenges all writers face: Jamey McCullers, Lynn Hallman, Glenda Loftin, Karen DuBose, Rick Werner, Edward Hallman, Debra Rosenblum, Martha Strawn, Bill Latham, Sarah Malinak, Edith Langley, Robbins Richardson, and Janet Bull.

And last to all of you struggling in a pressure cooker world with the insidious and misunderstood addiction

ACKNOWLEDGMENTS

ACKNOWLEDGMENTS

to work and life balance—a culture that seems to move us faster, more furious, and frenzied off the cliff of a sane and healthy life. May this book bring you the sweetness of doing nothing—moments to chill, live in the present, and savor your life to the fullest.

PRAISE

"Work addiction is an important and underestimated addiction. I'm truly grateful to Bryan Robinson for bringing it to greater awareness."

—TARA BRACH, AUTHOR OF *RADICAL ACCEPTANCE*

"There's a hunger we're trying to satisfy with substitutes for relationships that increase our isolation! Robinson offers essential help for all who are addicted to work or anything else!"

—HARVILLE HENDRIX, PH.D.,
AUTHOR OF *GETTING THE LOVE YOU WANT*

"Bryan Robinson offers insight, encouragement, and advice to remind us to focus on what's important in our busy lives. Reading each reflection is a step toward greater clarity, balance, contentment, and peace."

—MARK R. LEARY, PH.D., PROFESSOR OF PSYCHOLOGY
AND NEUROSCIENCE, DUKE UNIVERSITY

PRAISE

"Bryan Robinson has written a remarkable book on mindfulness. One of the greatest habits you can develop is to learn and internalize the wisdom of this book that can be effectively applied in daily life. I think anyone reading it will benefit."

—AMIT RAY, PH.D., AUTHOR OF *MINDFULNESS: LIVING IN THE MOMENT, LIVING IN THE BREATH*

"Only when I, like Bryan Robinson, was forced by one too many episodes of burnout to uncover childhood sadnesses did I begin to see work as an irreplaceable part of my life, but not the whole of my life. And only then did I begin to focus on what I could uniquely do instead of trying to do everything—thus beginning to be far more effective as a worker."

—GLORIA STEINEM

"Bryan Robinson is a leading-edge voice in the world of work addiction recovery. Born from his direct experience, these meditations are chock full of warm and powerful wisdom, guidance, and empathy. This frontline contribution helps us to recognize work addiction's corrosive effects on health, relationships, and livelihoods and to recover daily with more work/life balance. On a personal level, I am grateful to know that these many glimpses of wisdom are available for all of us who suffer from this quiet and so-called "respectable" addiction and for how I have been helped by Bryan Robinson on my own journey of recovery."

—ALANIS MORISSETTE

"If work is the axis around which all of your life turns and you don't prioritize anything above it, and if you risk losing your family, friends, and yes, even yourself, this book is definitely for you. Bryan Robinson is a wise fellow traveler on the journey to lead a balanced and fulfilling life."

—PEG O'CONNER, PH.D.,

PROFESSOR AND CHAIR, DEPARTMENT OF PHILOSOPHY

AT GUSTAVUS ADOLPHUS COLLEGE

PRAISE

ABOUT THE AUTHOR

Bryan E. Robinson, Ph.D., is a psychotherapist and award-winning author of two novels and forty non-fiction books that have been translated into fourteen languages. He is a contributor to *Thrive Global* and *Psychology Today* and has been featured on *20/20*, *Good Morning America*, *NBC Nightly News*, *The Early Show*, and *ABC World News Tonight*. Bryan maintains a private clinical practice and lives in the Blue Ridge Mountains with his spouse, three goldendoodles, and occasional bears at night. Visit him online at www.BryanRobinsonBooks.com.